I0074008

A MUST READ COMPLETE BLUEPRINT FOR USA SURVIVAL

(It is all here in this book, a complete blueprint that will guarantee the only chance for the USA to survive as a nation with individual freedom intact, period.)

FREE ADVICE ADD ON:

No one asked my advice, but I decided to give a little free advice anyway. There are two main ways to control or motivate people; it is through love or fear. Some believe love is best but fear is more dependable.

At least in the old days the west had sense enough to prop up strongmen and that kept order, but somehow along the way liberalism creep made that a no, no. Now, almost total disorder abounds, because the west to this day still believes one size fits all.

In many cases involving an army or fighting force it must boil down to option odds, meaning ones chances of surviving is equal or greater staying and fighting than running away. Strongmen shoot deserters on sight.

SIRMANS LOG: 15 NOVEMBER 2015, 0855 HOURS.

WORDS OF GREAT WISDOM:

What I keep trying to get through thick sculls is we must bring back a genuine true free market place economy, then the debt problem, the immigration problem, the health care problem, the crime problem, and every other grave problem we have will solve itself.

Only a true free market place economy has the power

1

to keep liberalism at bay, anything less is like pissing on a barn fire expecting to put it out. These politicians will be making promises until doomsday, yet higher taxes and more debt grows daily.
SIRMANS LOG: 09 NOVEMBER 2015, 1300 HOURS.

FOOTBALL PLAYERS DEMAND:
The purpose for going to school is supposes to be to get an education, period. How long can the USA remain a free people, duh? This is just another sad escalation of liberalism flexing its muscles; get use to it, much more to come.

With a problem of this sort in the final analysis it all boils down to a lack of societal discipline in some way. But, what can you expect, unless our arch-evil 1938 socialist minimum wage law is repealed it is impossible for the USA to be saved. We are now entering the early stage where only an iron fist literally can maintain order.

You can't keep individual freedom without self-responsibility, self-accountability, and self-restraint, period. Soon the people will demand that government take away our individual freedoms just to maintain order. Just keep living, you'll see. Liberalism is out of control and deadly.

There is no doubt in my mind that out of control liberalism is going to take the great USA down unless we get back to a genuine true free market place economy and soon. I wish I could break my pen and walk away from this, but it is a calling and I just can't.
SIRMANS LOG: 08 NOVEMBER 2015, 0045 HOURS.

NOTE:
The worst mistake any conservative with strong great character can commit is try to win the approval of liberalism, because if they can make you a perfectionist then you destroy yourself by dehumanizing yourself.

People don't love you because you are perfect; people love you because you are human. Never constantly deny any negative, make one statement per negative, then repeat that has been addressed and move on, period.

Remember, rightly or wrongly no one likes a whiner. Let them take a hike if they can't take a joke.
SIRMANS LOG: 06 NOVEMBER 2015, 0018 HOURS.

Lately I'm hearing a constant drum beat from conservatives and republicans on cutting taxes to save the USA from doom. Sorry, it is too late for that liberalism is much too embedded and powerful and will come roaring back with a vengeance if this path continues.

I agree under normal circumstance that should be the normal thing to do, but the masses upon masses of government dependents at the first sign of real pain politically is going to send conservatives and republicans packing.

The better and only way, again I repeat if conservatives and republicans have any chance of saving the USA from doom they must repeal the 1938 minimum wage law, then a true genuine free market place economy will kick in and do whatever it takes to save this great nation.

It is a one shot chance, if it is not taken or misses the mark, shallow minded liberalism will once and for all drive the final nail into our coffin, this I guarantee.

Only a true free market place economy has the power to bridle liberalism enough to have a fighting chance of saving the USA from total doom, period.
SIRMANS LOG: 29 OCTOBER 2015, 1754 HOURS.

BRIEF FOOD FOR THOUGHT ADD ON:
Sure, the rich and powerful has always aborted and killed babies in and out of the womb. But, as to the rest of society mass killing of future unborn babies in the womb is a modern thing within the last fifty years no matter the reason.

Nothing has advanced civilization more than conquering armies and in the distance past mass raping almost always was seen as just part of the reward bounty. Hell, even in slavery if every life that resulted from rape were aborted there would be a lot fewer blacks around today.

Yet, some blacks are setting on their high horses demanding that every life resulting from a rape be killed in the womb. Studies have shown that the trauma of being a raped victim in many cases is eased by the love from the innocent child. I'm not condoning anything, I'm just saying...
SIRMANS LOG: 27 OCTOBER 2015, 1938 HOURS.

What my harshest critics will never understand is no one acquires almost supernatural wisdom without enduring unusual great suffering to survive in some way, period. I feel if I weren't spiritual to the core I would have long fallen by the way side.

It is virtually impossible to mentally destroy anyone that can genuine love and forgive. I just repeat to myself as much as necessary, I can wish all people goodwill through God who strengthens me.

USA LEADERS FIDDLE WHILE ROME BURNS.
As a writer of almost supernatural wisdom I offer a USA survival blueprint why not follow it. If a better one exists, please disregard. Sure, You can laugh, but history will be the final judge. You have been enlightened, you know the one and only thing that must be done, now get it done.

Me, this little lone neurotic writer attacking this big giant liberalism Ogre is like David attacking Goliath. Don't look a gift horse in the mouth.

NOTICE:
I will almost always say bridle liberalism. The reason is liberalism is not necessarily a bad thing in fact liberalism makes a more caring and better world, but it will also destroy everything if not disciplined and kept under control. Either an iron fist literally type government or a government with a true free market place economy can keep liberalism bridled.

Since 1938 the USA no longer has a true free market place economy due to the government enforced minimum wage law. And without a true free market place economy the USA has no way to maintain societal discipline thereby allowing liberalism to take down this great nation.

5

These do-good make everything right liberals are on a warpath about gun control, they can barely sit still and are wiggling in their seats. What they don't understand and are too shallow to realize is out of control liberalism is the cause of the gun problem in the first place.

However, I'm one that believes liberals forcing threatening gun control down the nations throat is the one thing that will definitely give republicans a Trifectaor complete a Hat Trick in 2016.

If you want a better society you first must have a better class of people, period. From lack of societal discipline this USA nation is being over run with moral decay and culture rot, that is where the real problem lies. Almost all of this nations old tried and true norms and traditions have been corrupted by liberalism.

They have been replaced by new insane anti-survival norms like same sex marriages and mass killing of future unborn babies in the womb. I won't preach, I will end by saying you have been enlightened on what must be done to save the USA from total doom.

Gun violence is one of the least of this nation's problems, our way of life and survival itself is on a slow countdown. And here we are fiddling while Rome burns.

As a writer of almost supernatural wisdom I have said a thousand times the one sure thing that will save the USA from total doom, so there is no excuse why this great nation should go the way of the great Auk.

No matter which way the wind blows, I'm here to warn you that only a genuine true free market economy with no kind of government wage or price control can provide the discipline to save the USA and western civilization, period.

You see, only an economy without any kind of government wage or price control will have the necessary purging power not only to discipline and protect itself, but will also protect the nation's culture, moral, and spiritual values from over powering rot and decay like what is eating us alive today.

Repeal the arch-evil 1938 socialist minimum law now. Let the only thing that can possibly save the USA and western civilization, which is a genuine true free market place economy with no choking government wage or price controls, what so ever work its miracle.

Agree or not, like it or not, without a doubt I am right on this, I will bet the farm on it. There are certain things about human nature that never changes, things such as spite, envy, jealousy, hate, superstition, and the rest of our emotions. Things of this sort haven't changed one iota in over 2000 years.

Concerning societal discipline: As late as the nineteen fifties or sixties many small towns and rural areas in the USA didn't even bother to lock their doors. So, concerning societal discipline what has changed in today's world, the key word is discipline. The USA has practical no societal discipline left today.

That is the main reason we have so many nuts committing mass killings with guns today. It takes discipline to isolate or weed out those that won't conform. Sport teams use tryouts to see who conforms and the military uses basic training to see who conforms. Well, a healthy society on a much larger scale must have some means to isolate those unwilling to conform.

I believe those that has the mentality to go out in a blaze of hate and terror will always show some tell tale signs well in advance, its just that those that knows are not telling or speaking up. Many first grade school teachers to a high degree can point out even then the ones most likely to be in trouble with the law eighteen years later.

I will bet my bottom dollar that at least one person knew everyone of these mass killers was a danger to society in some way before they acted. The reason the USA doesn't have the societal discipline to isolate and deal with these type of individuals is because of our minimum wage law. Don't roll your eyes and laugh, because I know you think that is stupid and doesn't make sense.

Let me explain, the shallow minded see the minimum wage law only in terms of how much more money one is paid on a job and they can't get pass that. Sure, only a fool wouldn't like to make a living wage or make more money. And getting any kind of a private sector pay raise is a good thing and will work. But, on a large or national scale with everyone getting a forced government raise it may give everyone more money, but more purchasing power will be just an illusion.

It is an illusion because every forced government wage increase results in a higher cost of living increase. And over time the cost of living increases will far out distance any salary increases. The minimum wage law is why twenty years ago ones salary versus cost-of-living would buy far more in the grocery store then than it will today. And if moral decay and culture rot doesn't doom the USA first consumer cost of living soon will.

Buying power is what truly and really counts, not more and more lesser and lesser-valued inflated dollars, which the shallow minded and less informed can't seem to comprehend.

Yet, if the government raised the minimum wage ten dollars it would kill off most small businesses and consumer-cost-of-living would really sky rocket even more. Anyone that know the basics of true economics should know that any kind of government wage or price control doesn't work in the long run and will rip apart a nation's culture and moral inner fabric.

The real danger and destruction from any kind of government imposed wage or price control is what it does to the entire USA economy. Any kind of government imposed wage or price control de-nuts and renders a free market place economy practically helpless with almost no purging power left. Purging power is what gives an economy the discipline to protect itself, the nations culture, moral, and spiritual values.

Starting in 1938 the USA economy's hands has been tied behind its back due to the enacting of our minimum wage law, and ever since then the USA as a nation has been without societal discipline leaving the nation almost without a rudder.

Another big problem with the USA economy is the USA government is trying to manage and control it. That in itself is an impossible task simply because there is just too many variables. The government shouldn't be forcing a minimum wage on the private sector and it shouldn't be in the stock market either.

Plus, the biggest no, no of all is for government to ever become a social and family provider. Once that happens there is no peaceful way out for government, because when money starts running out the mobs is going to be coming after politicians with pitchforks. Only repealing the 1938 minimum wage law can prevent this from happening, otherwise there is not enough societal discipline left to keep western civilization from regressing all the way back to the stone age.

Government should run the country, the military and stick to collecting taxes and get the hell out of the way to allow a genuine true free market place economy to prevail. Government should stay with what it does best collecting taxes, running the country, the military, and leave the economy to the private sector, period.

Plus, that was mainly the way it was before government decided to take over private enterprise by not allowing the private sector to set its own wages and prices (The 1938 minimum wage law ended private control of the USA economy). And until control of the USA economy is back in the hands of the private sector it is impossible for this nation to survive, period.

As a writer with awesome creative thinking ability along with almost supernatural wisdom I believe even if the republicans do complete a hat trick in 2016 liberalism will still rule the day. In the USA and other welfare states around the world liberalism is on autopilot.

Which means the only thing that can bridle liberalism enough to save western civilization from total doom is a true genuine free market place economy, period. But, here is the catch; it is impossible to have a true genuine free market place economy with any kind of government enforced wage or price control in effect, period.

So, even if the republicans do get a Trifecta in 2016 by gaining control of both houses of congress and the presidency it won't save the USA from total doom, unless the arch-evil 1938 socialist minimum wage law is repealed once and for all.

The only true benefit I can see for a minimum wage law in the first place was to inflate our currency to finance and keep our liberal created welfare state in power. Without a minimum wage law a pure free market place economy will purge out inflation. Now, to change gears, Just like the life and death cycle is necessary for life to exist, the boom and bust cycle in an economy is necessary for an economy to exist. It is a law of nature.

The USA economy is going to collapse that is a given, no one knows when, but a big bust cycle is long overdue. My grave concern is what is going to happen afterward. I'm not out to scare anyone one, I'm just a lone writer with a one man's opinion, and hopefully I'm wrong.

It is just simply impossible for any society to get through a long overdue bust cycle without a strong nuclear and extended family system in place, which the USA no longer has.

Repealing the arch-evil 1938 socialist minimum wage law will restore our strong nuclear and extended family system along with strong morals and spirituals values providing time don't run out on us. Otherwise I can't see any way around total doom, period. You can call me crazy, a nut, or whatever, but that is the way I see it, sorry.

Before 1938 a lone woman with a purse could walk

through a black neighborhood or any neighborhood at midnight and no one would harm her. Today what has changed, the come about of the arch-evil 1938 socialist minimum wage law put a stop to societal discipline. And since that day our once real true free market place economy lacks the purging power to stop inflation, culture rot, or moral decay.

Lets face it, liberalism and its created welfare state has destroyed individual responsibility and accountability to the point that the USA may no longer have the capacity to remain a free people. In spite of out of control liberalism and its created welfare state we in the USA still has the most individual freedom found anywhere in the world.

Only the second amendment is keeping us free, but history is not on us gun owner's side. The arch-evil 1938 socialist minimum wage law must be repealed now, not tomorrow. Otherwise, one way or another big stud liberalism is going to eventually have its way with the 2nd amendment in my view.

ONE OF MY FACEBOOK COMMENTS:
I'm in favor of any union or the head of any company or corporation giving its worker's as high a salary as possible, which is a good thing. My whole argument is never should the government in a free nation force any wage or price control on private enterprise, that leave a free market place economy with no purging power.

That is the economy the USA has today, a phony weak powerless paper tiger that can't protect itself or this nations culture, moral, or spiritual values, period. This is why the USA has same sex marriages and mass killings of future unborn babies in the womb today, we have almost no societal discipline left as nation.

Facebook comment end.

PS:
Morally wise in the USA there is no telling what's next. With our phony weak P.... of an economy there is no societal discipline left to prevent moral decay from exploiting the very young, or limiting real men to just stud service and companionship. Twenty years ago no one would have believed same sex marriages would be legal and condoned by so many, either.
SIRMANS LOG: 05 OCTOBER 2015, 2120 HOURS.

RENOWN WRITER BREAKS DOWN IN TEARS AND LOSES IT
After writing this brief emotional article I had a strong urge to run it through my paper shredder, but decided to publish it anyway. I am a lonely neurotic uneducated self-made writer, and so many times I wonder, why, why O-Lord do I continue on writing when so many don't seem to understand or care what I have to say.

What is this force that drives me on, it seems so fruitless for me to continue on writing. Yet, I cry and continue on. I don't know what possessed me to write something as self-serving and wimpy as this article, I guess it is a force beyond me.

Almost every instinct in my body tells me what is the use, your writing is not liked or wanted, just break your pen and go away, you won't be missed. But, I just can't and won't, I have fought all of my life against self-pity and being a quitter.

Maybe this is why I am writing this article with tears in my eyes, I carry on. I'm one that believes positive

human effort is never wasted, who knows the lives I will never know that I may have touched and made a positive difference in some way, I carry on.
Thank you, thank you God for my life health and strength, I carry on.
SIRMANS LOG: THIS SUNDAY MORNING, 04 OCTOBER 2015, 1016 HOURS.

GUN VIOLENCE IN THE USA: THE REASON IN 3 WORDS BY RENOWNED WRITER?
I sum up the reason for gun violence in the USA in three words, "Lack of discipline", period. In fact there is no lasting enjoyment of anything in life when there is a lack of discipline. It doesn't matter, it can be love, sex, freedom, or anything you can imagine, without discipline it's going to become problematic.

Again, I will say this for the umpteenth time unless the 1938 USA minimum wage law is repealed the USA can't be saved. Nothing else can provide the discipline to stop out of control runaway liberalism from destroying this great nation, period.

There is really no need for me to say more, the USA is a free nation, only authoritarian nations can use the Iron fist to stop liberalism from destroying everything. It tends to be in the nature of liberals and liberalism to attack and destroy discipline. However, in the eyes of nature there is a need for everything in life including liberalism.

Sure, liberals are super aggressive and busybodies, but they makes sure Bambi is protected, plus this world would be a very, very dreary place without liberals doing good and trying to make everything right. They are sort of like greed and electricity, they can be very dangerous but the trick is never completely shut them down, just keep them bridled and under control.

In a free nation a non-phony true free market place economy will provide the discipline to keep liberalism bridled and under control. As to greed, there is no greater motivating force in our entire human makeup than greed. The main reason why communism and socialism will always fail is those systems of government tends to almost completely shut down greed.

Whereas, capitalism tends to let greed soar but still keep it bridled and under control by allowing free and unlimited competition. That is why in terms of production a free capitalist system will produce an over abundance of everything it needs and much more to sell.

The USA is not a socialist state yet, but with so many government dependents who knows what's next. Plus, the USA tax burden with countless government regulations is fast killing off what little greed motivation the nation has left. Expecting extra production in the future may become a joke.

More and more people want to just work and provide for themselves and family. They are saying to hell with hiring others and putting up with all of the government hassle and red tape non-sense. Small business and the mom's and pop's are the backbone of this nation, but our phony unreal non-free market place economy is fast wiping them out.

There can be no real true free market place economy with any kind of government wage or price control in

effect, period.
SIRMANS LOG: 02 OCTOBER 2015, 1923 HOURS.

DEADLIEST THREAT TO USA SURVIVAL...FIND OUT:
OK, here goes, I try to avoid doing this type of freethinking because many people already think I'm off my rocker. The older I get the more I understand why individual freedom is so rare through out history. There are just too many things in nature that makes individual freedom almost impossible to maintain.

Even the natural laws of nature such as "Taking the course of least resistance" will completely dominate our behavior unless strong unrelenting discipline prevents it. Nature is ruled by balance, which means everything in it is relative including survival.

There is no such thing as all good or all bad. Too much of a good thing is bad no matter if it's food, sex, or anything you can imagine, only balance keep things in line with the laws of nature. In my view the real core problem with the USA is not what almost everyone think it is.

I believe the core problem with the USA is unchecked and out of control liberalism, period. And until that core problem is dealt with everything else is an exercise in futility, period. The balance between conservatism and liberalism is almost totally one sided in favor of liberalism.

In my view the traits of liberalism are shallowness, softness, femininity, aggressiveness and a compulsion to do-good. After all liberalism does make sure Bambi, the needy, and the less fortunate all are protected.

But, strong no-non-sense kick ass discipline is needed to safeguard a nation and it's culture.

So, all of this talk of shutting down the government and making helpful changes in the tax code is an exercise in futility anyway in my view. The fact is until liberalism is balanced or brought under control it is a pipe dream to think about saving the USA.

Authoritarian countries use the Iron fist to keep liberalism under control. But, the only way to keep liberalism under control in free countries is to have a real true free market place economy to maintain a disciplined society due to individual rights. Enacting the 1938 minimum wage law in the USA took the bridle off of liberalism and year-by-year ever since liberalism has grown into this monster size political correctness cesspool that is engulfing us all.

The USA using an Iron fist is out of the question, so, the only way of stopping this monster to save the USA from total doom is to bring back a real true free market place economy, period. The only way for the USA to regain a real true free market place economy is to repeal the 1938 minimum wage law, otherwise the USA goes the way of the Roman Empire, period.

Unchecked liberalism will always eventually end up at the bottom of the barrel in the gutter, mostly because of too much love unbalanced with not enough discipline being taught to our young, just look around you. Today in the free world especially in the USA and Western Europe liberalism is on autopilot with a life of its own.

That means no matter the politics nothing can prevent liberalism from destroying modern civilization except one thing, I have given the answer to that through out my writing, so go figure.

Sure, Trump is shaking things up like never before, which is a good thing. This liberal induced welfare state has lulled almost this whole nation asleep.
SIRMANS LOG: 28 SEPTEMBER 2015, 1352 HOURS.

ADD ON #1
In a free nation the only major expense for government should only be for internal and external defense and the military, period. Otherwise it is like a nation feeding on itself with more and more people eating free with fewer and fewer people doing the providing.

This is the sad state liberalism has brought the great USA to today. How in the hell can any government finance the military for long when half the nation is feeding off government instead of being government providers. The reason this sad situation exist today is because ever since 1938 the USA has had a phony weak p…. of an economy with no biting purging power.

Ever since the 1938 minimum wage law liberalism has been able to inflate our currency thereby allowing government to keep adding more and more dependents to no end. There are some that don't think this is a bad thing, but they are wrong, doing this rips out the inner fabric of a nation and sends responsibility and accountability out the window.

Without enacting the arch-evil 1938 socialist minimum wage law the old pre-minimum wage USA economy would have purged out self-serving inflation. That would have prevented the liberalism baby from growing into this monster size destructive welfare state we have today.

I call on all men and women of goodwill with good judgment and sound mind, now you know what must be done, just go do it before it is too late. May God bless and keep the USA always. Amen.

I love liberalism when it is balanced and not out of control. But, when it is unchecked and out of control without a doubt it is going to destroy this great nation, period.
SIRMANS LOG: 30 SEPTEMBER 2015, 1739 HOURS.

DISSECTING THE USA ECONOMY BY FREDDIE L SIRMANS SR:
The biggest problem facing the USA and western civilization today is it's harder and harder to find men of super strong survival instinct that's necessary to have sound judgment like me. You can roll your eyes, but a hundred years ago 95 percent of the American population would have agreed with almost everything I write today.

But, today 98 percent of the population doesn't have a clue as to what I am talking about in my writing and think I'm some kind of dumb ignorant knucklehead babbling about a lot of stupid nonsense. That is especially true when I pound and pound about repealing the arch-evil 1938 socialist minimum law.

They think I'm some kind of a nut going around like "Chicken little" hollering the sky is falling and ought to just go away or be put away. Which means very, very few has the deep perspective to understand that economy-wise government forcing any kind of wage control or wage increase is like increasing the wing size on just one side of an airplane.

The economy functions properly dealing with it as a whole and to just deal with one side of the equation is just plain dumb and stupid. The fact is wages has a counter-part called consumer cost of living, and to keep and maintain a healthy economy those two items must be kept in balance.

Otherwise, the cost of living in the form of inflation is going to eventually collapse that economy along with destroying that nations culture, moral, and spiritual values, too. The only way to keep and maintain a balance between wages and consumer cost of living and keep inflation at bay is to never allow any kind of forced government wage or price control.

Yet, this very basic simple fact is beyond all but a very few today. I'm paraphrasing, when I say, "What good is it to gain the entire world but lose your sole". That is my view on what has happen to the good old USA, we have allowed the shallow minded liberal to install our phony economy and create this welfare state that has made a lot of people fat and happy. But, we will soon lose this great country unless the 1938 minimum wage law is repealed now, not tomorrow.
SIRMANS LOG: 20 SEPTEMBER 2015, 2049 HOURS.

CONCERNING THE CLIMATE CHANGE MYTH:
During the September 16, 2015 GOP presidential debate one of the candidates said something that I hadn't thought of on this climate change thing. I'm paraphrasing but he basically said as I understood it that if the liberals succeeded in taxing businesses and raising a lot of money, it wouldn't actually be spent on protecting the climate.

They would find a way to use that money to grow government and finance even more social programs. So, that got me to thinking about this whole climate change matter.

The liberals are well aware and knows that giving out goodies is the only thing keeping them in power, so now it all makes sense to me with money getting tight new ways to squeeze the tax payers must be found. And what better way than insanely pushing climate change as a secret cash cow that will keep liberalism fed.

Who can argue against a more healthy and safer climate? Now, it is all coming into focus and making sense to me on what is really going on, here. When has liberals ever put the health and survival of this great nation above grabbing and keeping power, If that was so in my view they wouldn't be hell bent on taxing and spending this nation out of existence, duh.
SIRMANS LOG: 17 SEPTEMBER 2015, 1302 HOURS.

CURRENT EVENT, CHRISTIAN LADY IN JAIL: Sure, the USA is a nation ruled by law instead of man; I for one believe the law must be upheld under all conditions and at all cost, period. Catalyst, catalyst,

catalyst, there is something called human nature, and right now in the great USA moral decay and culture rot is a bigger threat to USA survival than even economic doom in this writer's view.

Repeal the arch-evil 1938 socialist minimum wage law and let a real true free market place economy save this great nation before it is too late. I double dog dare the USA to act now while we still have a chance to save a hundred million or more lives.

Be aware, this writer believes this Christian lady in jail has the potential to light a huge gay backlash fuse if she is not somehow freed from jail, the overly severe punishment is creating a Christian Martyr. That is just this writer's opinion.

Now a few words about the Trump effect: What I like about Trump is he is a man of action and I would vote for him in a New York minute. This drip, drip, by drip with everyone standing around watching liberalism bury this great nation alive I feel is the worst possible way to go out.

The real skinny on this is my personal view is Trump can't save the USA, in fact no individual or movement can. The only thing that can possibly save the USA at this late liberalism engulfed stage is a real pure free market place economy. And all it will take to get a real pure free market place economy is to repeal the 1938 minimum wage law, period. Duh.
SIRMANS LOG: 06 SEPTEMBER 2015, 0816 HOURS.

WILL USA SURVIVE COMING COLLAPSE VERSUS BACK TO THE STONE AGE

As a great creative writer with almost supernatural wisdom so many times I have felt that my writing is totally ignored. But, deep down I know that can't possibly be true. Sure, after nearly eighty years as a welfare state for the most part in the USA sound judgment accompanying a strong survival instinct may be in question.

I have no way of proving it but I believe around the world some may see my writing as the gospel truth. Also, I believe around the world some may see the USA as like an injured wild beast, which is the most dangerous thing there is.

Despite all of the USA culture, moral, and economic problems without a doubt everyone around the world knows even with a declining image this North American giant is still the most powerful military and economic force on earth. A free nation demands from its citizen's responsibility and accountability, otherwise at some point the iron fist will not be denied.

In my view it is a given the USA economy will soon collapse no matter what action is taken, and I pray that I'm wrong on this. My grave concern and purpose is to help save as many as possible through the collapse and past it. And to do that the must thing is to get the government as much as possible and as soon as possible out of the family provider business.

It is critical that we get as many people as possible back to depending on themselves and their fellow man as soon as possibly. The fact is very simple when the full collapse hit the USA government won't have the means to take care of anyone and will be lucky to be able to maintain order.

When I plead and I cry to repeal the arch-evil 1938 socialist minimum wage law, that law in itself has no power, but it is the key that will unlock and free up a real true free market place economy. And a real true free market place economy is one of the most powerful things on earth.

It will give back power and survivability control to the people so when the collapse hit and government can't provide, the people can survive on their own. Nothing is going to stop this coming collapse, but a real true free market place economy is the only thing that can give the USA a fighting chance to survive through it.

Otherwise, for the great USA it may mean back to the Stone Age. Failure to heed my great almost supernatural wisdom advice on this is beyond my power or control, so let the record stand, I did my duty, so be it.
SIRMANS LOG: 02 SEPTEMBER 2015, 1951 HOURS.

ADD ON #1
Sure, before the arch-evil 1938 socialist minimum wage law the USA had many problems, but culture rot and moral decay was not one of them as it is today. Before 1938 the USA had a real true free market place economy minus our evil liberal enacted socialist law giving government the power to set wages and prices

over all private businesses in the USA.

In one swoop that arch-evil socialist law destroyed the right of the private business sector to control its on destiny by being able to set its own wages and prices. By losing that right and power the USA economy lost its disciplining power to purge thereby leaving the economy with no way to weed out waste and inefficiency, including liberalism.

What we have today, as an economy in the USA is a phony weak pretender that is powerless to defend and protect itself or the nation's culture, moral, and spiritual values. Without repealing this evil law quickly the USA will soon be left with millions upon millions of helpless dependents that will die due to a collapsed penniless USA government.

I dare you, prove my prediction wrong. God help us.
SIRMANS LOG: 03 SEPTEMBER 2015, 1617 HOURS.

ADD ON #2
The economic boom and bust cycle is part of nature just like the life and death cycle. No matter how good the medical care sooner or later the grim reaper won't be put off any longer. The time is up and the collapse (bust cycle) won't be put off much longer.

Our human responsibility is to be prepared to survive through the cycles and it can't be done without a strong nuclear and extended family system. No society or civilization has ever survived without a strong nuclear and extended family system, period. And right now the USA nuclear and extended family system is in almost total ruins.

Repealing the 1938 minimum wage law will restore the USA nuclear and extended family system but the problem is there is so little time left before this collapse hit. Lord help us.
SIRMANS LOG: 04 SEPTEMBER 2015, 0957 HOURS.

ADD ON#3
Another thing I've decided to comment on is this shallow minded liberal technique of trying to entrap people by asking gotcha questions. Sure, most everyone knows that being informed is very important when running for political office. But, do the shallow minded liberal asking that type of question truly understand why there is a need to have libraries, I doubt it.

Only a fool is willing to clutter his/her mind with all kinds of needless details. In terms of leadership it is far more important to have the ability to know where and how to find what one needs to know than to try micromanaging things.

I think the best thing is to just say up front, I'll answer your questions but I'm not here to take a quiz, then stand your ground because going down that road places one in a no win situation.
SIRMANS LOG: 04 SEPTEMBER 2015, 1518 HOURS.

USA: TO ACT, OR NOT TO ACT AND DIE.

Talk, talk, talk, liberalism and the welfare state it have created continue to nail the lid on the USA coffin. The older I get the more I am convinced that by and large people are going to do what they can get away with. All of this culture rot and moral decay liberalism has brought upon this great nation will never be cleaned-up with just talk, talk, talk.

It all starts with how we raise our young, period. These perpetrators that are committing all of these horrendous crimes was never conditioned to fear punishment for wrongdoing when being raised. The more one has to earn and struggle for life the more precious and valuable life becomes. That is a fact and there is no way around it, yet liberalism totally disregards and ignores this fact.

These perpetrators has never been conditioned to respect other people's feelings and property, all they know is me first, I want mine, I want it all and any consequences is the furthest thing from there mind. So, until liberalism is bridled and brought under control the great USA will soon be history. And I will bet the farm on that. Action is what it is going to take to save this great USA the land of almost unlimited individual freedom.

One way or another we as a nation must act and get the ball rolling no matter right or wrong. Repealing the arch-evil 1938 socialist minimum wage law will definitely get the ball rolling no matter right or wrong because the worst thing is not to act at all.

If the action is proven wrong the nation will be forced to correct that wrong because any action is better than

to do nothing but talk, talk, talk. It is not about this writer being right or wrong it is about the survival of my beloved homeland, period.
SIRMANS LOG: 01 SEPTEMBER 2015, 0017 HOURS.

PS: TAKE HEED: AN OLD BIBLICAL TRUTH, "Blessed are the meek, for they will inherit the earth". Writer's injection: Remember it said the meek would inherit the earth not the weak, like the now predominant liberalism victimized USA has become.

In fact I believe that is one of the reasons Trump is so popular he stands up to liberalism and faces it down. In my view liberalism is an aggressive destructive form of existence and is just like all threatening intimidating boogie man type facades.

All one has to do is stand your ground and face it down and it will retreat as just pesky noise with no bite.

GUNS VERSUS A FREE USA!
Myself, I am nonviolent and believe in nonviolence except in cases of self-defense and personal protection. However, I thank God for the USA's second amendment and this nation's citizens right to bear arms.

I believe freedom and the citizen's right to bear arms goes hand in hand. And if you take away the citizen's right to bear arms it won't be long before government nips individual freedom in the bud. Sure, the USA may have more gun deaths than any other nation but it also has far more individual freedom than any other nation, and that is why so many is trying to get here.

The core USA violence problem is not the gun, The gun has not all but totally destroyed our culture, moral and spiritual values, or left us with a phony weak p.... of an economy. No, it is liberalism riding shotgun with its created welfare state that has brought the great USA to its knees, and will finish us off unless the arch evil 1938 socialist minimum wage law is repealed.

Many years ago in rural areas and small towns guns were everywhere and a multiple killings was something almost unheard of. Back then most people never even bothered to lock their doors at night or anytime, so, what has changed, liberalism. Because back then about the only place you could fine a liberal was in a rich family or maybe on a collage campus, and almost never was a liberal to be found among the poor.

Bam! Then came the "New deal" fortified with the arch evil 1938 minimum wage law and since then liberalism has never looked back and to this day is about to drive the final nail into our coffin. Today practical the entire poor is liberal with an entitlement mentality and killing more future unborn babies in the womb than any other group, God help us. In my one man opinion I believe the real culprit is liberalism and its created welfare state, period.

Liberalism has corrupted so many people judgment that few can recognize a moral threat or have the wisdom to know what real compassion is. Almost everyone today is doting on their children and spoiling there pets while letting strong discipline and self-sacrifice teaching go by the way side. Our children are

100 percent of the nations future and how we raise them is everything if the nation is to survive.

How can you expect someone to be responsible and accountable with self-restraint when they have never been raised and conditioned to be that way, you can't. I for one think medical supervised flogging ought to be considered for young law-breakers, but that type of thinking today is seen as extremely cruel and uncivilized.

Sure, it will cause some sore Asses and hurt feelings but it wouldn't kill anyone. It would save ten times more of our ill raised youngsters than our correction systems is saving today and wouldn't have to house and feed anyone. Yet, compassion like everything else today is upside down. Especially the poor and so many others are just not raising our young to be law abiding and productive future citizens today.

When nuts with a gun go shooting and killing up people it is because they are so self-centered that they hardly know what a self-sacrifice is and has never been conditioned with self-restraint when young on how to deal with personal frustrations, period.

There is more than one way to skin a cat, and I'll admit that my cold hard tough love may be too much, but we are losing this great country and rescuing the young is a must, this writer just can't look the other way. Again, I say get the ball rolling by repealing the 1938 minimum wage law now that is the USA only chance of coming out of this fix alive. I ask in your name, God save this great land of individual freedom.

The Trump Impact In 2016

SIRMANS LOG: 27 AUGUST 2015, 1350 HOURS.

ADD ON #1
More about the Trump effect: Demographics, demographics, demographics, that and scientific polling is what the establishment and political promoters lives on. I for one believe depending on that only will never enable them to ever understand the Trump effect.

Everyone knows the establishment and others are waiting and hoping for the Trump movement to self-destruct or peter out, and the sooner the better. I believe because of human nature they may be in for an awful long wait.

Sure, with modern scientific polling pandering to demographic groups has become an art that the so-called political experts have used very successful in the past, but it is not an advantage against Trump.

There are some demographics percentages that are not going to vote republican under any circumstance and on the other hand some demographics percentages are not going to vote democratic under any circumstance. However, at heart we all know right from wrong whether we admit or not. And we all know Trump is definitely telling the truth with the things he is saying.

So, I will wrap this up by saying: Trump is going over the heads of demographics and appealing directly to truth, decently, and the people's self-interest. And that is something that can't be dismissed as just a passing fad.

So, the people are only choosing realness, truth, decency, and self-interest over fake, pandering, selling out, etc.

Liberalism has brought this great nation to this sad state, repealing the 1938 minimum wage law is the only thing that can bridle liberalism and bring back some sanity to this nation, period.

SIRMANS LOG: 28 AUGUST 2015, 1432 HOURS.

ADD ON #2
This writer believes African Americans will never support Trump on a large scale. I believe Trump has a good chance of doing very well with all minorities except African Americans. My reasoning for believing this is African Americans in my view have never shed its slave dependency mentality.

Due to this dependency mentality in my view African Americans see the Democratic Party as its livelihood provider instead of feeling responsible for its own survival as individuals and as a community. And that loyalty bond can't be broken its like a child's dependency on its parents for survival.

The only way this locked-in dependency can be shed or overcome is for African Americans to be forced to stand on there own two feet. But, our destructive liberal created welfare state will never force anyone to be truly responsible and accountable let alone be forced to stand on there own two feet.

SIRMANS LOG: 29 AUGUST 2015, 2306 HOURS.

THERE IS AN OLD SAYING:

"No guts. No glory". This writer for one is so glad to see someone come along that in a positive manner takes this saying to heart, because that is what it is going to take to defeat liberalism, which has all but totally destroyed this great nation.

In free societies only a true free market place economy can keep liberalism at bay and under control, unlike in an authoritarian society that uses the iron fist to control liberalism. Almost every crime or vice imaginable in the USA is running rampant and the law can't even keep drugs out of the prisons let alone stop hardly anything else.

The most powerful thing in a free society is not the law but a true free market place economy. The USA economy today is not real or true but a phony weak P…. A true free market place economy can't exist with any kind of forced government wage or price control in effect; anything else is phony and unreal, period. Before you can get control over culture rot, moral decay, crime, vice, and the like's first liberalism must be faced down and subdued.

Right now in the USA liberalism is out of control. And the only way to save the great USA is to get liberalism back under control by repealing the 1938 minimum wage law. Fiddling with the tax system or anything else is an exercise in futility; liberalism will see this great country in hell first before it will slacken its death grip on this great nation.

SIRMANS LOG: 21 AUGUST 2015, 1555 HOURS.

The pundits and talking heads are all over the map on why the Trump Express seems to be at cruising speed and even extending its lead. The lead reason they are saying is the public wants non-politicians and new comers. And to some degree I think there may be some truth there.

However, I think it is something much more basic that Trump is exercising here. I think Trump is only displaying good character and being man enough to stand up for his true beliefs. In my view it is just that simple which earns genuine trust and respect from the people even if they disagree with his tactics.

In this day of scientific polling almost every politician is pandering to the people and they know it. So when a man comes along with the issues and the moral high ground at his back that strong character shows through and people trust and respect that.

The people knows Trump is not pandering, he is teaching and educating which makes a world of difference to the people on an emotional level. I'm not going to get all long winded on this matter. I think this whole Trump phenomenal boils down to just strong character, which too few seem to recognize today.

Before the arch-evil 1938 socialist minimum wage law destroyed the USA true free market place economy our economy would kick ass and that kept liberalism at bay and under control. That is because any wage or price control handicaps a free market place economy where it no longer has the purging power to discipline itself or the people.

Now liberalism is out of control and almost no survival tools are left to save this great country. The road to hell is paved with good intentions, but human beings are not motivated by good handout liberal intentions they are motivated by a response to reward or punishment.

You help someone help themselves otherwise you create a dependent and mentally destroy a good human being sometimes for life. Liberalism and our welfare state have all but totally destroyed this great predominant Christian nation.

It is impossible for the USA to survive very much longer unless this 1938 minimum wage law is repealed. With my almost super natural wisdom I can be wrong on a lot of things but without a doubt the must to get rid of the evil 1938 socialist minimum wage law is not one of them.

No country can survive very long with government providing for more than the military and a very few other essential services only, it is just impossible. The evil minimum wage law allows for government to inflate the currency and provide for its own destruction.

This evil 1938 socialist minimum wage law must be repealed for the USA to survive, otherwise the USA collapses back to the stone age, period.
SIRMANS LOG: 14 AUGUST 2015, 2317 HOURS.

ADD ON #1

I understand it but 98 percent of the American population doesn't that it is impossible for the USA to survive much longer with government as a super provider welfare state. So, the key is a way must be found to get the American people back to being providers for themselves.

Repealing the evil 1938 socialist minimum wage law will in a controlled manner start that process of empowering the people back in charge of their own survival. And I have the God given wisdom to know until this wolf in sheep clothing free market place wage control killer is repealed nothing can save the USA no matter what anyone says or does.

You can take what I say with a grain of salt or you can take it to the bank, but I guarantee you history will prove me right on this. Sure, much of what I write is to the extreme and tough love, but I am all about survival baby, not just feel good policy and going the way of the Great Auk.

SIRMANS LOG: 14 AUGUST 2015, 1154 HOURS.

ADD ON #2

I, great writer Freddie L Sirmans Sr. see Trump as a great trailblazer. Reminds me of "Give-em hell," Harry! A supporter yelled "Give-em hell," Harry! Truman replied, "I don't give them hell. I just tell the truth about them and they think its hell". That is what Trump is doing just being unafraid to tell the truth. I say give-um hell, Trump!

The Trump Impact In 2016

Sure, Trump is blazing a huge trail and USA politics will not return to just the same old business as usual in my view. However, as a writer of almost super natural wisdom I repeat, the cold reality is the USA is far past the point of no return morally, culturally, and financially to be saved unless a miracle occurs.

When a house foundation is decayed and rotten to the core that house can't be saved unless it's foundation is rebuilt from scratch. The USA house foundation nuclear and extended family system is in almost total ruins and there has never been a society that survived with that being the case.

We have same sex marriages and mass killing of future unborn babies in the womb as the norm. We have over 95 percent of the USA general population looking to government as their savior when it doesn't produce one red cent. The financing of everything the government has or gets was seized from the private sector.

The only guaranteed thing that can possibly save the USA at this late stage is to repeal the arch-evil 1938 socialist minimum wage law. But, only a miracle can make that happen when 98 percent of the USA population fail to understand the 1938 minimum wage law is a wolf in sheep clothing and a free market place economy killer.

In my view ever since 1938 the USA economy has been a weak powerless P.... with no purging power to discipline itself or the nation all due to the evil 1938 minimum wage law. God save the great USA.

SIRMANS LOG: 15 AUGUST 2015, 1131 HOURS.

ADD ON #3

Here is another thing, Trump is perceived as bigger than life. Look at how people worship Hollywood and the Stars. There is just something in our human makeup that causes most of us to be impressed with power and individuals that seems bigger than life.

It reminds me of what some of the early American evangelist's discovered and said: Those like Father Divine and others discovered that as a rule being just plain and ordinary no matter how good your message was it would not get you a great following.

But, on the other hand as a rule when one projected an image of expensiveness, a lot pomp and extravaganza with flashy dressing and cars it tended to result in a much bigger following. There seems to be something in the human spirit that attracts them to things bigger than life.

Just Look at the Brits, No one beats the British in ceremony, pomp, extravaganza, and that sort of thing. And this little island nation single-handed ruled almost the entire world for many years. So, I'm telling you human being loves this bigger than life stuff. People and nations that are good at this sort of thing pack an awesome wallop.

In my view never count someone like Trump out. Plus, the secret and power behind all of this is: There is no better way of teaching and learning than through ceremonies and rituals, especially for the young, they just eats it up and soaks it all in. Look at the effect rap has on the young, they see the star's as bigger than life.

SIRMANS LOG: 16 AUGUST 2015, 1730 HOURS.

IS ARMAGEDDON NEAR???
CAN A MIRACLE SAVE THE USA FROM TOTAL DOOM?   INTELLIGENCE VERSUS RAW WISDOM
I don't know why I had the urge to write this article. Maybe it is out of frustration more than anything else. Even though I know I am right, still sometimes I wonder and have doubts about my God given wisdom and sanity in terms of what I write and believe.

This thing they call judgment thinking has somewhat haunted me ever since childhood. The ability to separate self and emotions from a problem and bore through fog and side issues right to the core has been with me ever since I was a young child.

Even when I hoed vegetable rows on our farm as a ten or eleven year old my dad and older sister Betty would criticize the way I did my rows. They would say why couldn't you hoe your rows like ours. Even then I did things in an organized and systematic way and to me my rows looked and seemed to be better but they disagreed.

Even today with the books I write I know ninety five percent of the USA population will never believe or understand what the hell I'm writing. It is not because my writing is complicated it is just the opposite, many people see most of my writing as simple nonsense babble and even stupidity.

The Trump Impact In 2016

Many years ago I read a book and can't even remember the title or who the author was but I do remember the author talking about meaning. He went on to say just a dot on a piece of paper may not mean anything to others looking at it, but the meaning and wisdom behind who put it there may have took a life time (paraphrased).

As to my self, I'm not educated, brilliant, or highly intelligent, in fact I'm the slow plodder type, but once I understand the basics my slow climb takes me high up on the mountain top. And I definitely understand's the basics of an economy, which the USA general population does not.

I think anyone with any depth and even a weak survival instinct knows that our great USA is in serious survival trouble with eighteen trillion in debt.

The problem is can the USA be saved with our individual freedom still intact. However, not everyone thinks the country needs saving, especially liberals. I'm one that can't figure out if liberals are shallow because they are liberal or liberal because they are shallow.

Anyway, many a liberals have become conservative over night when a mugger slammed one up side the head or some other dreadful thing happened to one personally. Otherwise, what's happening to someone else can't seem to get through to his or her shallow brains.

Now, back to simple things that sometimes have a deep meaning like the dot I previously mention. Here is a short sentence that I have dwelled on for the last two years or so and what several of my latest books are about.

The sentence I'm talking about is: The arch-evil 1938 socialist minimum wage law must be repealed. Maybe I'm a fool, dummy, idiot, or just plain stupid, but I for real believe the 1938 minimum wage law paved the way for the doomsday welfare state the USA have today. The come about of the 1938 minimum wage law is what has caused the destruction of the nations moral, spiritual, and family values.

Here is the reasons behind my beliefs on this minimum wage law: From a pure economic understanding point of view there is no way a true free market place will allow inflation or a welfare state to get off the ground. A true free market economy has the ability to reset back to zero wages and prices and purge out inflation and without inflation a welfare state can't get off the ground.

You see, a true free market place economy is 100 percent totally controlled by the private sector, period. Bartering and trade is the foundation of every private sector economy and adding a currency takes it from there.

In hard and troubling times, especially during the great depression there was a mixture of bartering and currency use, many doctors were paid with farm products. But, in my view the main advantage of a free market place free of government control is the economy has discipline power through purging to reset back to zero if necessary.

A merchant couldn't charge more than the consumers had the ability to pay and stay in business. Sure, before the minimum wage law came along the system had many problems. You had the boom and bust cycle coming along every seven years or so, but what those that lack wisdom failed to realize is nature must have a way to purge out and get rid of moral decay and culture rot.

Now, after nearly eighty years moral decay and culture rot is so powerful that without a miracle it may take going back to the Stone Age to get rid of the waste and rot. Before the 1938 minimum wage law not only did the USA economy purge out financial waste and rot it protected our moral, spiritual, and family values, too.

In 1938 the last of the "New deal" programs was enacted, the Fair Labor Standard of 1938 (FLSA). Wham! In one stroke for the first time in the USA existence an economy that had always been 100 percent able to operate under private control, now all private property rights, business production, and business distribution has flipped to 100 percent under government control.

There-after all wages and prices paid would be what the government said they would be. The minimum wage act took away the USA economy ability to reset back to zero thereby eliminating its purging power to discipline itself or the nation. Ever since that day the USA economy has been too weak to safeguard the nations culture, morals, and spiritual values.

The Trump Impact In 2016

By destroying the USA economy's ability to reset back to zero and purge out inflation the shallow minded liberals was free to tax and spend to kingdom come. Now the liberals with very little resistance has by taxing and spending made so many government dependents and left the nation 18 trillion in debt only a miracle can save the nation from total doom.

Still, I love-um all they are good Americans its just that they shouldn't be in charge and running things, period. However, even with a miracle the only way the USA can possible be saved is to first repeal the arch-evil 1938 socialist minimum wage law, period.

I don't believe nothing else no matter what it is can save the great USA until first this arch-evil minimum wage law is gotten rid of once and for all. That is just the way it is, sorry, I call it as I see it.

There is no long time survival for any nation with same sex marriages, mass killing of future unborn babies in the womb, and endless means of birth control galore. Don't shoot me the messenger, I don't make any rules, Mother Nature does.

Order, order, order, we have just about lost our great USA when far too many people today justify physical resisting law enforcement. Sure, there are some abuse and always has been, but never forget civilization cannot exist without law and order first and on the spot. Take up your grievances later.

Our doomsday welfare state has made far too many

people feel like kings unto themselves with special entitlements and pampered treatment. Armageddon must be near.
SIRMANS LOG: 28 JULY 2015, 2305 HOURS.

HAVE RINO'S SECRETLY TAKEN OVER THE REPUBLICAN PARTY???

I BELIEVE THE RINO'S IN HIGH PLACES AND GLEEFUL LIBERAL MEDIA IS JUST ABOUT FED UP WITH "THE DONALD." AND WILL TRY TO TAKE HIM DOWN AT ALL COST.

GOP INFESTED WITH RINO's: ANOTHER PREDICTION BY THIS GREAT WRITER MAY COME TRUE.

FIRST SOME WORDS OF WISDOM FROM THE GREAT WRITER AND THINKER.
Tax, tax, tax, naive, naive, naive, is I the only one left with any real wisdom, here. Flat tax, value added tax, sales tax, and on and on, but the fact is it really doesn't matter which tax system is better or worse. No tax system can support a welfare state or any government in the role of social and family provider very long.

Government survives on profit by taking it from the private sector. It takes profit from the private sector in the form of taxes or seizes property and auctions it off for the profit. Government has the power and once government becomes a social and family provider its going to take what it needs as a provider no matter what form of tax collection system it uses.

The fact is government should never become a permanent social and family provider in the first place. Sure, temporary government assistant as a last resort is not a threat, but to make it permanent is a poison pill.

The founding fathers did everything possible to erect barriers to limit the size of government, but once government becomes a super provider it pays the cost to be the boss. Economically speaking, boom and bust cycles are natural and comes with the territory.

That is why a strong nuclear and extended family system, good moral and spiritual values, and adequate emergency bartering capacity with many, many small farmers and home gardeners are a must.

Any nation with the above mention tools in place can withstand and ride out any bust cycle until a new boom cycle kick in. But, God help a nation without those tools when the bust cycle hit, it could mean back to the Stone Age. The boom and bust cycle is part of nature the same as the life and death cycle.

Sure, man is able to delay the cycle but nature dictate at some point the cycle must be completed, and the sad part is the longer the delay the more severe the bust cycle will be. And anyone that thinks I'm off my rocker is a fool in my view.

Even at this late stage a true genuine free market place economy can work miracles, but, a minimum wage law bounds and gags an economy and takes away it's power to discipline itself. Unless the USA repeals the evil 1938 socialist minimum wage law the

USA has no chance of surviving the big bust cycle looming on the horizon.

Almost everyone thinks the law is the most powerful thing in a free nation but it is not, the economy is the most powerful thing in a free nation. The reason we have morals, values, and the inner fabric of the nation coming apart is because the USA has had an unreal phony inflated P.... of an economy ever since the arch evil 1938 socialist minimum wage law was enacted by the liberals.

Without the minimum wage law a real genuine free market place economy would have through purging protected the nations proper norms and traditions. Today our norms have become extreme and perverted, ISMDH (I shake my damn head). And that leave our young, which is 100 percent of our future totally unprepared for survival.

Sure, the USA has always had severe problems throughout its existence but never was its culture and family values ripped apart until after the evil 1938 socialist minimum wage law bounded and gagged the real USA economy.
SIRMANS LOG: 01 JULY 2015, 2317 HOURS.

GAY MARRIAGE UPROAR: GREAT WRITER SPEAKS BRIEFLY ON THE MATTER
Ok, Ok, I see and hear all of the uproar about gay marriage, but the fact is it matters very little either way because the USA and western civilization is doomed anyway unless a miracle takes place. What

most people don't realize is there is a proven reason for all norms and traditions.

There is a reason why every society known to man has rituals and ceremonies. Until our welfare state came along in the USA our norms and traditions were well maintained and protected. Anyone like me with a strong survival instinct knows without being told that survival of the species is totally 100 percent dependent on the young and unborn.

Therefore rituals, ceremonies, marriages, norms, and traditions all are for the raising and teaching of the young. And there has never been and never will be an institution more suitable for the raising and teaching of the young than marriage under the umbrella of a nuclear and extended family system.

Anything no matter what it is that threatens this evolutionary process is a threat to human survival. And if man fails to protect this evolutionary process, Mother Nature will definite step in soon. And mother nature's way of dealing with the situation is resetting modern civilization back to the Stone Age, we'll find out soon. The USA is living on borrowed time, economically-wise, morally-wise, and spiritually-wise.

In the USA mostly liberal hogwash is the norms being instilled in our young today, which makes it impossible for this great nation to survive very much longer, period.

Once our welfare state became a super social and family provider it never gave a damn about maintaining and protecting proper norms and traditions. And now here we are today in the great USA with a generation of citizens that don't know their ass from a hole in the ground in terms of raw bare bone survival.

The only thing that can save the USA is to repeal the Arch evil 1938 socialist minimum wage law. That in itself won't directly save the USA, but it will start a process of getting rid of our inflated phony economy so a true free market place economy can kick in and allow the people to take back control of their lives.

I could analyze much, much more but enough said, I think you get the point.
SIRMANS LOG: 27 JUNE 2015, 2220 HOURS.

SUPREME COURT RULING ON SUBSIDIES WAS ACTUALLY A GOD SEND TO THE REPUBLICAN PARTY EVEN IF THEY WON'T ADMIT IT
I will make this very brief, there has never been a society headed toward total financial collapse that has ever changed course, power concedes nothing and always goes down with the ship.

Recognized or not, it is a fact that it is impossible for the nation to afford Obamacare, yet we proceed on. You can't get blood out of a turnip, and you can't have health care for long when very, very few can afford it.

The Trump Impact In 2016

In the grand theme of things this latest Supreme Court decision really doesn't matter because the USA is far too far down the socialist road to be saved without a miracle anyway.

In life there is really no such thing as free, one way or another everything has a price even every decision we make.

This recent Supreme Court decision about subsidies was actually a blessing in disguise to the Republican Party, because this insane Obamacare debacle is very soon going to start dishing out a lot of dreadful financial pain, but the scheming irresponsible liberals won't have the Republican Party to blame and kick around on this due to the supreme's ruling.

The USA economy is already on the brink of a total collapse with 18 trillion in debt and there is no possible way our economy can survive Obamacare in my view. The USA is doomed as a free nation unless our arch evil 1938 socialist minimum wage law is repealed. But, we have 98 percent of the nation thinking the minimum wage is not only a good thing but the only thing that matters and ought to be raised.

The only solution to save the USA at this late moral decay and culture rot stage is to get rid of the minimum wage law entirely and to have no wage or price controls what so ever, then the free market place will be free to set it's own wages and prices without the heavy hand of the government thumb on the scale.

Otherwise, this whole USA and world economy is going to soon collapse and take us all back to the Stone Age. All of that being said, as for the USA, only a divine act of God can bring about a repeal of this arch evil 1938 socialist minimum wage law. Glory be to God. Long live a free America. Hallelujah.

Political I am an independent, but I see the Republican Party as the only hope of saving the USA from total doom. After the Supreme's recent ruling on subsides to me it looks like the stars, the Gods, and destiny itself are all pointing to a republican Trifecta win in November 2016.

And if that does happen the republicans will have the power to once and for all repeal and put a dagger through the heart of this arch evil 1938 socialist minimum wage law. I believe that is the only thing that can save the USA and western civilization from total doom.

However, they think I am a total nut case, and right now the odds are 100 percent they will never do something like that. Never the less if they do win a Trifecta in November 2016 no one can ever say the republicans never had a chance to save the USA and western civilization from total doom.
SIRMANS LOG: 25 JUNE 2015, 1154 HOURS.

IS THIS WRITER A BLOOMING IDIOT OR A MAN OF GREAT WISDOM? TRUE OR FALSE, MAKE YOUR COMMENT AT THE BOTTOM.

The Trump Impact In 2016

As a great writer, deep thinker, and unsung super achiever I feel more and more of my predictions are beginning to come to past.

Especially my constant drum beating to no end that any minimum wage law is evil and means death to a true genuine free market place economy. But, it is like a lone voice hollering in the wilderness, everything falls on deaf ears, no one is interesting in taking my bitter medicine.

The USA, Greece, Western Europe, and much more of the world uses the minimum wage to inflate currencies and prop up phony economies. A phony economy is the only way a welfare state can survive because without a minimum wage law a true free market place economy will purge out inflation and keep it out.

I'm not going to go into details on the damage the minimum wage law does to a free market place economy in this article, that can be found in the many, many books I have written. No one asks me and no one is going to take my advice anyway. However, my advice to all welfare states is get rid of any minimum wage law now before it is too late.

When everything collapses it will be too late then except back to the Stone Age. With no minimum wage law in place the people are free to open millions of small businesses, hire each other, trade and barter with each other, and in effect save themselves and the nation, too. Right now in the USA and other welfare states that is impossible, too much red tape.

The minimum wage law is only the first of thousands of laws, licenses, permits and other road blocks unimaginable. Today in the USA almost everyone is depending on the government or someone other than self for his or her survival. And the people are going to be lost when big government, big business, and this colossal welfare state soon collapses.

The first problem is 95 percent of the USA population doesn't believe that something so unimaginable can happen. It is not only going to happen, but I'm here to tell you it is not as far away as we think. No one knows the day or hour when the collapse is going to occur but to the wise all of the signs are present now.

Greece is only the tip of the spear in my view.
SIRMANS LOG: 23 JUNE 2015, 2213 HOURS.

SPARE THE ROD YOU SPOIL THE CHILD!
I, Freddie L Sirmans Sr. as a writer of almost supernatural wisdom believe that is just as true today as it was 2000 years ago. On this article I'm writing I haven's done any research and don't feel a need to on the things I am about to say. I already know there is an exception to everything in life no matter what it is.

In general as a rule my statements will hold true enough, and that is good enough for me. "You raise up a child the way he/she should be and when he gets older he will not depart, and if he should stray most likely at some point he will return to his raising."

Why should anyone expect a child to be responsible and accountable when he/she has never been conditioned to be responsible and accountable? There is nothing that will instill a stronger conscience in a child than carpal punishment, but it should only be used fairly and as a last resort.

Today we have people committing suicide in some cases almost at epidemic levels. Today we have far more people committing horrendous crimes and murder. Today we have far too many people growing up on all kinds of mind-altering drugs, both legal and illegal. And I could go on and on.

However, I see one common thread going throughout all of these sad situations. That common thread I'm speaking of is very few if any of these people growing up ever felt the sting of hard lick on their ass for improper behavior.

Disagree if you may, but the fact remains, human beings respond and is motivated by reward or punishment and talk is only rhetoric. Plus, good and evil is just two sides of the same coin. I rest my case. **SIRMANS LOG: 22 JUNE 2015, 0143 HOURS.**

WRITER BELIEVES WITHIN THE NEXT 17 MONTHS THERE WILL BE AN ALL OUT LIBERALS ASSULT ON THE 2ND AMMENDMENT.
Don't be a fool, don't be a fool, and don't be a fool! The liberals are on the brink of totally destroying the

greatest, richest, freest, and most prosperous nation to ever exist.

In my view they have just about destroyed the USA by creating our welfare state. But, a welfare state could never have survived this long without first depending on a phony inflated currency.

When the liberals enacted the arch evil 1938 socialist minimum wage law that blocked the economy's ability to discipline itself by being able to freely purge and reset wages and prices back to zero. Of course no one is going to work for zero that would be slavery, but the seller and buyer should set wages and prices never the government.

Thereby without the economy's ability to purge inflation and reset prices and wages back to zero the liberals have been able to tax and spend and inflate our currency to no end. This 1938 evil law in one sweep for the first time gave the federal government absolute power over all United States private property rights and private business production and distribution.

Thereafter, the government would have the final say on all price and wage transactions in the nation, private or otherwise. The real miracle working power in a free market place economy is its purging ability to get rid of waste and inefficiency regardless of who you know or b... The minimum wage law acts as a purge inhibitor and leaves a free market place economy with no way to protect itself or the nations culture and morals values.

Beginning with the enacting of the 1938 minimum wage law the USA economy could no longer purge out inflation. That is why ever since the 1938 minimum wage law the USA has slowly been going to hell in a hand basket. Now, every kinky and negative anti-survival special interest group imaginable is out of control and running wild.

They now have the coalition power to bring this great nation to its knees. Almost eighty years after the enacting of the 1938 minimum wage law only one tiny thread is preventing the liberals from administrating the final coup de grace. Except for this last tiny thread the liberals today would destroy the last bastion of true individual freedom left in world today.

That tiny little thread I'm talking about is the 2ndamendment. And I believe within the next seventeen months the liberals once and for all are going to pounce for a kill to try to take away our guns. Will the Gods allow it to happen, we'll see.

I will sum up by saying this: If I had to pick just one thing as the cause of the USA coming destruction, It would be the enactment of this arch evil 1938 socialist minimum wage law. And I don't believe anything can save the USA until this law is repealed, even if no one else believes that except me.

Nothing on earth has the power to produce jobs, wealth, and abundance like a true kick ass free market place economy. Repeal this evil 1938 socialist minimum wage law to set our economy free again to set its own wages and prices not the government.

Repeal this evil law and save this great USA nation, for Christ sake, people. Hallelujah!!!
SIRMANS LOG: 19 JUNE 2015, 1430 HOURS.

WHAT WAS THE FIRST THING GEORGE WASHINGTON SAID WHEN HE RODE UP TO THE WHITE HOUSE: WHOA! WHAT WILL BE THE FIRST THING THE ESTABLISHMENT WILL SAY WHEN THE TRUMP EXPRESS ENDS UP AT THE WHITE HOUSE: HOLY COW, UNBELIEVABLE! SIRMANS LOG: 12 AUGUST 2015, 2044 HOURS.

HAVE RINO'S SECRETLY TAKEN OVER THE REPUBLICAN PARTY???

CAN THE REPUBLICAN RINO'S AND GLEEFUL SOCIALIST LIBERAL MEDIA STOP THE TRUMP EXPRESS???

WHAT DO YOU THINK OF THIS WRITER'S ANALYSIS???

THE TRUMP PHENOMENAL:
I, Freddie L Sirmans Sr. man of great almost supernatural wisdom and deep deep creative thinking has decided to weigh in on the Trump presidential candidacy. As a self-made writer I very seldom comment on individuals.

However, I think Trump entering the 2016 presidential race is so profound that it has the potential to shake up politics in this nation more than anything in the last century. And a word to the wise, not taking this man serious may be the biggest mistake anyone can make.

The Trump Impact In 2016

I believe his candidacy is going to effect the liberals and democrats even more so than the republicans, simply because he has the issues, moral high ground, and headwinds all at his back. Which means the more the predominant liberal news media attacks him the bigger and more popular he will become.

But, my guess is the liberal news media will avoid attacking him head-on issue-wise and instead pound away on pretending he is not a serious candidate and whatever he says is not to be taken seriously.

In my view the liberal news media just steam rolled over the last three republican presidential candidate losers, but now they have finally in their eyes met a foe that will stand toe to toe and refuse to back down, high drama pending.

No pun intended, I think Trump is not a man to "Beat around the bushes. I think Trump is not afraid and is going to constantly, no pun intended, beat the bushes. And if nothing more beating the bushes" long enough will eventually drive the political snakes from both political parties out into the open.

Also, I believe its going to make it a lot harder for the RINO's to hide their true colors. I see some republicans already becoming very emotional when talking about Trump. I believe if Trump doesn't cave like the last three republican presidential candidate losers he is going to make believers out of a lot of people including me. I never though he would ever run in the first place.

And another thing, they are going to hound him to no end on details, which is a trap because if he is suckered into that they got him. Everyone knows the Dem's are going to promise the moon and back and tax and spend to kingdom come, but when have they ever gave details in advance?

Instead of trying to pander to the poll results republicans need to stand for what will save the country and focus on educating the public. I know without a doubt that the republican base and most of the country will never vote against someone totally committed to lower taxes, more jobs, and strong national defense, period.

Instead the republican candidates in the last three presidential elections has tried to out pander the liberals, which is scatter brained thinking in my view. Limiting and dwelling on three or less things then people get it, but chasing votes you'll never get and being all over the map means no one knows what you are selling or what you really stands for.

It is all about building and turning out your base, the Dem's know this, that is why they keep winning presidential elections.

Reality is reality and fact is fact, and the reality and fact is Trump is saying a lot of things a lot of people are agreeing with. That concludes my analysis.

I give the Dem's credit for the fact they have no shame or regret when going down holding on to what they believe in, they double down and there is never any talk of changing into something they are not concerning their base.

On the other hand, there should never be any shame or regret for the republican party going down fighting for lower taxes, more jobs, and strong national defense. Instead the Republican Party is trying to be all things to all people, which end up pleasing no one, and leaving the base with candidates they don't trust except the lesser of two evils.

Now, on a personal basis, I don't want to end up begging on the streets, but I will go down holding on to what I write and believe in even if no one ever agree with me. A many of times I have felt cursed with wisdom that no one but me seems to see. And I have wondered why do I keep preaching to deaf ears.

No one seems to be interesting in my bitter medicine, yet there is a drive to fight on for my survival and that of my nation. I don't know if it is destiny, fate, or insanity, but, deep down in my soul I feel some way some how my seemingly wasted effort is not in vain **SIRMANS LOG: 17 JUNE 2015, 1531 HOURS.**

PS:
I see the anticipated coming drama and excitement with Trump in the 2016 presidential race as very refreshing. However, I feel I must add my own belief as a writer of almost supernatural wisdom for the record.

Until the evil 1938 socialist minimum wage law is repealed I don't believe it is possible for the great USA to be saved, period.

PS#2: "THE DONALD RIDES AGAIN."

PS#3:
One may not agree with "The Donald," but the political process in the USA may need shaking up. The USA is 18 trillion in debt and our economy could collapse at

any moment. Our nuclear and extended family system is in ruins. Our good moral and spiritual values are in ruins.

We have no emergency back-up bartering capacity with small farmers and home gardeners to survive on and regroup-with if the economy collapses, or any big disaster strikes. If anything big and bad happened to the USA it could be the end because we have let the welfare state destroy all of our must tools for human survival.

Who knows why something's happens. The good "Lord works in mysterious ways." Repeal the arch-evil 1938 socialist minimum wage law or the USA perishes.

I don't know and no one else knows why this "Trump" phenomenal is so powerful and dramatic, but, one thing I do know beyond a shadow of doubt is only a miracle can save the USA from total doom. Is there some kind of fate or destiny message in all of this high drama?

During the Great depression: The USA nuclear and extended family system was strong, reliable, and healthy. The USA morals and spiritual values were good, solid, and above reproach. The USA had masses of small farmers and home gardeners that provided enough emergency back-up bartering capacity to feed and save the nation.

However, this time around we are left with practical none of the above mentions must have survival tools. I believe the iron fist will be used to kill millions just to bring about order, but even that won't be enough due to no survival tools left to rebuild with. Back to the Stone Age may be the final destination.

This is all fiction and the exercise of my overly active imagination, please dismiss.
SIRMANS LOG: 19 JULY 2015, 142 HOURS.

PS#4: You know what Dick Nixon said when one of his sidekicks was caught misbehaving, "sure, he is an S.O.B. but he is our S.O.B." And I doubt there will be any serious changes in the polls involving the McCain case. The whole USA political process is being shaken-up to the very core, and we'll all just have to wait and see what eventually comes out in the wash. God save the good old USA.
SIRMANS LOG: 20 JULY 2015, 2241 HOURS.

WRITER FREDDIE L SIRMANS SR. CRIES OUT IN PAIN FOR THE FUTURE OF HIS BELOVED COUNTRY THE USA.
It is so sad what the welfare state and liberal news media has done to this great nation the USA. Order, order, order, and more order, it is impossible to have an orderly and civilized society without order.

Our liberal induced welfare state has turned much of the USA into a needy greedy, self-centered, uncivilized, unforgiving, and ungrateful people in my opinion. It just confirms what most people with real wisdom already knows, if one doesn't have to struggle for it, life and everything in it becomes cheap and taken for granted.

Self-sacrificing and some time giving up a right for a wrong is becoming rare and rarer, now, it is all about me, me first, I want mine, I want it all, what kind of society has we become?

Most of the young today has never faced cold tough hard discipline that demands obedience now, no sass, and no back talk, just obey and act now. Our welfare state has allowed a false reality to come about in this great nation and now the piper must be paid, and believe me we as a nation is about to pay dearly in blood, sweat, and tears. Just keep on living we'll see.

I believe the USA and western civilization itself is in the final stages of their life ending cancer-ridden welfare states. Enough said, no one want to hear my bitter medicine, I will leave you with this: In my view no form of government has ever existed that was more self-destructive than a welfare state.

Not even a pure communist or socialist state completely destroys the very foundation of human survival itself like a welfare state does, given enough time a welfare state will totally destroy the nuclear and extended family system and leave no tools in place to rebuild upon. The USA and much of western civilization is past the point of no return. God have mercy.

In the end a welfare states leaves almost nothing to rebuild upon, it leaves the nuclear and extended family system in ruins, it leaves good moral and spiritual values in ruins, and it leaves no emergency bartering capacity with small farmers and home gardeners to speak of. No tools, practical nothing is left, its literally is back to the Stone Age.

SIRMANS LOG: 15 JUNE 2015, 1356 HOURS.

PS:
Anyone that thinks that our own welfare state wasn't somehow behind the recent hacking of government personnel files must believe in the tooth fairy in my view.

SIRMANS LOG: 12 JUNE 2015, 1001 HOURS.

NOTE: UNCONSTITUTIONALLY BUREAUCRATIC LAWS ARE BREEDING CONTEMPT FOR THE LAW ITSELF.
Respect and obeying the law is extremely important for the survival of a free nation. Yet, we have a law that punishes one for how they withdraw their own money from the bank.

I think that kind of a law breeds contempt and disrespect for the law itself, period. Sure, no law is going to please everyone, but what happen to its better to let the guilty go free than to punish one innocent individual. What has we become, has the almighty dollar took over our souls.

TOO MANY REPUBLICANS TODAY ACT MORE LIKE WANNA BE DEMOCRATS.
The attack dog liberal news media has shamed republicans off of the three things that have always won them presidential elections. The three things are lower taxes, more jobs, and strong national defense.

The founding fathers designed this great country as a

republic for those seeking elective office to educate the people on what is in the best interest of the survival of the country, not to surrender to phony polls on what greedy, emotional, uninformed, and irrational voters want.

A true statesman will go down fighting for what is right for the survival of his/her country, not just to gain or keep power and let the country go to hell in a hand basket. Folks, don't hate me for what I believe. Let me explain, politically speaking I am a freethinking independent.

I didn't set out to favor any one political party my sole interest is acknowledging the best chance of the USA survival as I see it. Forgive me, but with the liberals and democrats I see no chance of the USA surviving. Again, forgive me, still with the conservatives and republicans I see almost no chance of the USA surviving, but even with a flicker some hope exist.

The fore mention three things are very simple and may not seem important in today's debt ridden welfare state, but they are still republicans winners. If Dole, McCain, and Romney had locked on to them three simple things I believe they would have won.

The liberal news media can't defeat one that locks on to lower taxes, more jobs, and strong national defense. And they will never attack these three things directly, but will instead pound away for details and try to brand one as mean and uncaring, only a statesman can withstand the pressure.

The Trump Impact In 2016

Anyone advocating lower taxes, more jobs, and strong national defense should never be suckered into giving details, because everyone knows the Dem's are always going to tax and spend and when have they ever given details in advance.

One may not agree with the democrats but one thing is for sure, everyone knows what they stands for like it or not, they stands for bigger government and more social spending, and gives the middle finger to our soon to be $20,000,000,000,000 debt.

On the other hand, right now if you ask anyone what the last three losing republicans presidential candidates actually stood for, duh, no one knows. That is the problem with the Republican Party today, it lacks a core belief of trust for people to make a strong choice and fight for it.

Unless someone is prepared to make an iron stand on three or less things and not let the liberal news media keep them all over the map 2016 is going to be another loser repeat. It is a given the liberal news media is going to brand anyone that doesn't start promising goodies as mean and uncaring.

Who says people won't vote for you unless you answer every silly or unnecessary question the liberal news media may ask, no comment will get my vote every time. One can't be everything to everybody and expect to survive the liberal news media, because for every republican they are the real opponents.

With the persistence and determination of the liberal news media only an iron will can keep one locked on to lower taxes, more jobs, and strong national defense, which has always allowed republicans to win presidential elections.

Many years ago just like the democrats everyone knew exactly what republicans stood for, lower taxes, more jobs, and strong national defense. Now, the republicans acts more like wanna be democrats and is going to lose again in 2016 unless they return home to basics.
SIRMANS LOG: 30 MAY 2015, 1509 HOUR.

The all over the map strategy is already starting, and unless a republican limit at all cost to lower taxes, more jobs, and strong national defense 2016 will be a lost cause. Focusing on side issues like entitlement issues, voter fraud, illegal immigrate driver license, and other like stuff to the Dem's is like throwing a rabbit in a brier patch.

That keeps the focus off of the dire condition of the economy, lack of jobs, insane medical cost, and sky-high daily cost of living, duh. And I wouldn't be one bit surprised if the republicans fall for it again in 2016.

I must give the liberals credit, they may be shallow but they are smart enough to know that the republicans cannot defeat them for the presidency by trying to solve the entitlement-spending dilemma. And they are right; it is a fool's game in terms of becoming president of the USA.

The liberal news media will make sure the general

public is kept economically ignorant and will fight tooth and nails to keep them that way. The sad part is we are going to lose our freedom and this great nation and the republicans do have the sense to know it if something is not done.

Whereas the liberals are too shallow or selfish to realize the danger and will readily go down with the ship just to gain or keep power. Lord knows, I hope I'm wrong, but I believe the USA economy is on the brink of collapsing for real.

I believe it is a given, it is going to happen, nothing is new here, everything dies or collapses at some point, otherwise there couldn't be rebirth and growth and life couldn't exist on earth.

The wise thing for the USA to do if it wants to survive past this coming collapse is free up and untie the USA economy from the evil 1938 socialist minimum wage law, that will give us a fighting chance to survive. That is the only way the people can take back charge of their lives and with a true genuine untied free market place economy nothing is impossible, freedom and the nation will survive.

If the republicans win a trifecta in 2016 they will have the power to repeal this evil 1938 socialist minimum wage law and save the last bastion of individual freedom left in the world. Otherwise, it may be another 10,000 years before individual freedom see the light of day again.

I believe the Gods are smiling down on us for this last

great hope for individual freedom, it must come to past, or else.
SIRMANS LOG: 06 JUNE 2015, 0020 HOURS.

NOTE: Who really knows, there may be a divine reason how a neurotic mentally handicapped cripple misfit almost single handed can crawl out of the wood works and seize the pulse rate of this great north America giant, then sound the distress call alarm for its survival. That is no ordinary task. Hallelujah.
SIRMANS LOG: 08 JUNE 2015, 1011 HOURS.

NOTE: IS A COLLEGE DIPLOMA A MUST TODAY?
The old folks used to always say; the biggest fool of all is an educated fool. And adding my opinion I think anyone that thinks a college diploma is a must to reach the pinnacle of success in today's world is a fool.

Sure, it is an advantage to have a college diploma, nobody can deny that. Plus, in certain medical and technical fields especially the S.T.E.M fields (science, technology, engineering, and mathematics) its true a college diploma is a must. But, other than that it's not that big of a deal, and even the technical skills needed can be hired when one has the money and knows what he wants.

Two of the greatest computer pioneers to ever exist were not engineers, but they knew what they wanted and got it. Enough said.
SIRMANS LOG: 25 MAY 2015, 1513 HOURS

WESTERN THINKING VERSUS MIDDLE EAST REALITY:
OK, I'm going to make a very brief statement on what I think is military common sense. In every military war or conflict there are going to be people wanting to desert or run away. I think in every army it is a death sentence to desert during time of war.

Now, that being said, it takes cold harsh brutal discipline in many cases to make the odds of surviving better fighting the enemy than running away. Many armies have used divisions behind the line to shoot on sight anyone running back to safety.

I believe in certain parts of the world with many tribal and other factions only a strongman can do what it takes to make his army fight instead of running away. And until the west realizes this fact the whole thing is an exercise in futility in my view.

That is my one man's opinion; I said the same thing during the Iraq war and haven't seen noting since to change my mind. However, crying over spilt milk concerning the Iraq war serves no useful purpose and is a sign of irresponsibility and weakness.
SIRMANS LOG: 24 MAY 2015, 1724 HOURS.

<u>FINAL SOLUTION TO THE RACE AND ECONOMIC PROBLEM IN THE USA AS SEEN BY GREAT WRITER FREDDIE L SIRMANS SR., A MUST READ.</u>

UPDATED VERSION: AFRICAN AMERICAN EXCUSES, EXCUSES, EXCUSES, AND I'M SICK AND TIRED OF IT. WRITER ATTACKS BLACK LEADERSHIP.

Halt, stop, or brace yourself, because this great writer is fixing to let her rip, go on a tirade, rant, or what ever you may call it. OK, lets just dispense with any bull s... and just talk plain turkey. Sure, there is a lot of racism in America, always has been and always will be. Hell, I may be called a racist, but I think not.

Life is not perfect and this nation is not perfect, but it is the greatest country to ever exist in my view. I love this great country and it is the only home that I have ever known. This great country offers the most individual freedom and opportunity to ever exist on earth, and it still does in spite of our beloved tax and spends liberals, but still I love-um like a brother.

Now, as to my beloved African American race, the problem with us is too much pampering, period. Hell, I'm a neurotic mentally handicapped cripple from my childhood bed wetting days, yet I will never stoop to being just a plain excuse maker. If one accepts excuses for failure an excuse can always be found.

Sure, there may be be a good reason for an excuse, but as for my self I don't want to hear it, I only accept results. Like a coach once said: "you show me a good loser, and I'll show you a loser." I have been counted out all of my life. For me, I have always taken responsibility for my own survival and I know beyond a shadow of doubt that otherwise I wouldn't be standing today.

Today all I hear from African American leadership is what we lack, what we don't have, we don't have jobs, and on and on. However, the question that needs to be asked is: What do we need to do for our community our selves? Duh! And they will all look at each other like helpless sheep. Number one should be how could we provide more of our own jobs in our communities.

We African Americans have our racial priorities mixed up or maybe even misplaced in my view. Everyone's priority should be immediately family first, then community, city, state, country, but ones race can never be totally ignored to fit somewhere in that order.

One must have a mental identity to know who he/she really is as a person; otherwise one could end up with no true racial identity. Something of the sort has happened to the African American race on a mass scale.

We African Americans as a race mentally see ourselves as dependent like siblings that can't do for ourselves and must be taken care of by the master. And like most siblings we are jealous and compete against each other for the master's favors. That is why you see the herd mentality and we always vote anywhere from 90 percent to 99 percent for one party in almost every election.

We as a race are locked into this dependent sibling psyche. It is not a bad thing, it kept the African

American race alive in an almost totally hostile environment right out of slavery. However, circumstance and the nation has evolved and that type of psyche is no longer needed The only thing that can break this dependency chain is for African Americans to be forced to stand on its own two feet. Folks, I don't have anything to do with reality, I am only telling things as I see them, you have the freedom to totally disagree with anything I write and brand me a fool and idiot, so be it.

The African American race in America is awesome; we hold many of the most powerful elected offices in this great nation, from the office of president on down. There is no logical reason why African Americans can't employ at least a quarter of the jobs in its own communities, yet I doubt its over 3 percent.

For God sake, grow up African Americans, grab the bull by the horns, and learn to love all people and especially those that look like you. Now, don't you go telling me you don't have hate and contempt for those that look like you? Otherwise, why else would there be all of this mass killings in black communities?

Plus, where you spend your money proves where your first loyalty priority lies and it's certainly not with the man in the mirror. No one is expected to support a dirty greasy spoon eatery, but remember Auburn Avenue and the likes in other cities could equal the best before the welfare state came about. Now, our elites run as far as affordable away from an all black neighborhood and it is all because of our welfare state.

The welfare state has reduced the once proud Negro race to a bunch of government dependent siblings that are constantly at each others throat. We don't trust each other or truly respect each other and is ashamed of an all black neighborhood. And don't give me this bull excuse about high crime, the movie "Raising in the sun" proves blacks couldn't wait to get out long before crime was a problem.

If you don't love who you really are how can you expect other races to respect you. Liberalism is responsible for this sad condition and to this day still patronizes African Americans and hates nothing more than a black that's wants to be self sufficient and independent. A black conservative threatens liberals ability to keep African Americans dependent minded and self-rejecting more than anything else.

You black man, you don't truly love your own people, you mentally see yourself like your master and better than that sassy nigger that is undeserving of respect. Besides, you see that sassy nigger as a competitor against you, why should you kiss his ass and help him to get ahead, f... him, I'll spend my money where I want too, and anyone that's got a problem with that can kiss my black ass. This is the type of thinking that goes on in the minds of so many in the African American community.

The only thing that can break this locked-in African American dependency mentality is to kick the young eagle out of the welfare state nest, then it will be forced to fly on its own, that is what the mother eagle does. What I just said is not cold and uncaring, that is being prepared to survive on ones own, and not disappear off this earth when this welfare state soon crashes.

The African American sad condition is the tip of the USA survival spear, or the canary in our culture mine. God save my beloved homeland. Hallelujah.

OK, OK, having aired it out and said my peace, what is the real solution to the African American problem? Anyone familiar with my work should know my constant drum beat for the only thing that can save all of America and even western civilization.

It is the economy, fool! Nothing on earth is more powerful than a genuine true free market place economy; it trumps the law and everything in terms of having and maintaining an orderly society.

However, the USA liberal socialist destroyed our true free market place economy almost eighty years ago by enacting the evil 1938 socialist minimum wage law. And the inner fabric of moral decay and culture rot along with a lack of any emergency bartering capacity has grown unabated ever since.

A true free market place economy must be absolutely free to have the power to discipline itself and the nation, the same as Mother Nature, with its supreme law of natural selection. There must be a survival need for anything in nature to exist, otherwise it starts ceasing to exist based on nature's supreme law of "Natural selection."

The enacting of the 1938 minimum wage law gave the USA government for the first time absolute power over private property rights and business production and distribution. That act for the first time allowed liberals to seize almost absolute power by operating a candy store and promising the moon and back.

Before the 1938 minimum wage law it was almost impossible to inflate the USA currency because the economy had the discipline power to purge out inflation, waste, inefficiency and the likes. Now, the minimum wage law acts as a purge inhibitor and every imaginable negative anti-survival special interest group in America have grown like wild flowers unabated ever since. Mass killing's in the womb and same sex marriages are just new additions to the anti-survival paths the USA is going down.

Negative anti-survival special interest is now a swamp with the coalition power to take down this great nation. Creating our minimum wage law purge inhibitor is like trying to stop nature's life and death cycle, insane. The evil 1938 socialist minimum wage law have an almost over-powering appeal to the economically ignorant, and has all but destroyed our culture, good morals, and any capacity to barter.

A nation can't have emergency bartering capacity without enough small farmers and home gardeners, which is what got the USA through the great depression. I could go on and on with the destruction this evil 1938 socialist minimum wage law has done to this great nation.

But, I will wrap it up by saying this: Everybody and his brother has an opinion, but it is my God given destiny to let you know until the 1938 minimum wage law is repealed it is impossible for the USA to be saved. The "Final solution" is to repeal this evil law, or we perish, period.

I believe all to no avail the federal reserve and politicians trying to save this welfare state beast will eventually sell the nations sovereignty, land, wealth, and mineral rights off like a hooker on the block. Plus, there is no telling what has already been sold off being $18,000,000,000,000 in debt already.

Only a handful of people know, but I seriously doubt there is any gold left at Fort Knox anymore. I can't make anybody believe me; still I believe I understand the workings of an economy as well as anyone. And I promise you this weak phony P.... of an economy the USA have today is almost as useless as tits on a boar hog in terms of saving itself or this great nation.

Repeal the 1938 minimum wage law and give the USA economy back its original power, please Sir/Madam. It is not about how much increase in wages that really count, it is about having a job to buy enough food and necessities to survive at all. What good is a higher wage if you can't afford hardy anything, duh? It won't happen overnight, but repealing the minimum wage law will wean inflation out of our currency so $1.00 will buy what $20.00 will today.

Folks, I don't have to be right on my assessment, and I even hope I'm proven wrong. Why oh Lord, why have I been blessed with so much raw wisdom, it is like a curse, I see things so clearly, why me o-lord. Writer answers that himself: Why not you. Amen.
SIRMANS LOG: 07 MAY 2015, 1328 HOURS.

LIBERAL SUICIDE SPENDING
This is a subject I decided to revisit. There is a conservative faction that wants to bring about a states convention to demand the government balance it's annul budget.

On the surface having a convention to do that sounds reasonable and maybe ought to take place. Twenty years ago I probably would have jumped on the bandwagon. However, I have evolved and now realize liberalism has no boundaries or limits to what it will go to keep over spending.

Today I think any convention of the sort would more than likely cause a total disaster. The first reason is it wouldn't solve the problem. Our welfare state beast is ignoring the constitution and the law now and just adding new laws are not going to make this beast change its ways. The next reason involves human nature.

Liberals tends to be far more intelligent and smarter than conservatives but as a rule are shallow surface dwelling thinkers. The conservative's advantage has always been their focused staying power and deep sound judgment. However, there is a world of difference between today's conservatives and those in the founding fathers days.

Ever since the "New deal" and the come about of our welfare state conservatives has become almost as moral corrupted and shallow minded as liberals. It is a waste of time to pass more laws trying to force liberals to control spending.

They have weak survival instincts and respects no threats in spending from here to kingdom come. But, never forget liberals are not dumb or stupid, when giving up any of their own money they are the stingiest of any group. What it actually boils down to is they struggle with not being selfish to a fault, and that includes spending other people money.

Most conservatives are self-bound by morals and emotional boundaries such as guilt, shame, etc. Where as liberals tends to be far less restricted when going after something they truly want. Nothing that is within the law is going deter a liberal lion/lionness from grabbing power and keeping it.

Power is what this liberal suicide spending is all about. Social spending keeps liberals in power and no amount of morals; love of the country, or anything legal is going to stand in their way of holding on to power. Many liberals tend to be aimless but you give a liberal a cause or a goal and you got an almost unstoppable force on your hand.

If the great USA is to ever get control over suicide over spending from the liberals it can only be done with a physical barrier. So, here we go again, that means repealing the 1938 minimum wage law. Enacting that law is what took away a government-spending barrier in the first place.

That law gave liberals absolute power over private enterprise and private property rights and enable them to tax spend inflate, tax spend inflate, tax spend inflate in a never-ending upward spiral. In fact I don't believe its possible for any free nation to remain free very long with liberalism and liberals at the helm.

Freedom and democracy demands a responsible and self-controlled populace to last over a hundred years in my view. The liberals seized complete control over USA private business enterprise and private property rights with the enacting of the 1938 minimum wage law.

Unless that law is repealed this nation will never remain free to 2038 let alone more than a hundred years since the law was enacted.
SIRMANS LOG: 04 MAY 2015, 2107 HOURS.

BALTIMORE SUPER MOM: I HAVE A DIFFERENT VIEWPOINT ON THAT MATTER. WHAT DO YOU THINK?
In fact this writer is out of phase with almost everything that goes on now a days. I take no joy in raining on anyone's parade or stealing anyone's thunder. I'm referring to the mom being praised for

slapping her young son around and the news media even talking about making her woman of the year.

First let me explain my views on raising a well-balanced disciplined child. I believe corporal punishment is a supreme act of love in terms of long-term survival. Nothing instills a stronger conscious in a child than corporal punishment. A child raised with a balanced of love and discipline have by far the best chance of long-term survival.

I believe, used, as a last resort corporal punishment is a far more powerful form of love when raising the young. Many times the young will hate the one that gives them hard tough discipline. Today far too many parents see a child as a love item to be doted on, which I think is a terrible way to raise a child.

A child is a separate individual that should be taught responsibility and accountability to be a productive citizen many years later. Instead today many parents try to always please the child to make the child love them, which I think is a self-centered irresponsible parent.

The child that hated the disciplinarian most of the time years later will thank God for the only one who gave him the tools to survive. You see this intense almost spiritual like love many youngster years later will have for a hard nose strict disciplinarian sports coach. Now, back to the Mom that was slapping her kid around, God bless her.

I may disagree with her method but God bless her

heart for caring and doing the best that she knew how to protect her child. I'm one that thinks a parent should never use their hands to discipline a child and especially a teenager. With parents of old that would be a complete no, no.

I believe when using corporal punishment and as a last resort one, two, three, or what amounts of licks should always be announced first. There is an old axiom that says: "A general should never give an order he knows will not be obeyed." And by the same token I don't think a parent should ever give a child corporal punishment unless he/she knows it will administer a fair amount of pain.

Otherwise, corporal punishment without pain just breeds contempt and disrespect. Just like when a mother tells a kid fifty times "Don't do that," to me in a reverse way that is actually teaching disobedience. The most important thing in child raising is consistence then the child will know what to expect.

But, when a child is allowed to disobey fifty times and on the fifty first time the parent is in a bad mood or fed up and backhand's the kid off a chair, that's no way to raise a child. Back to the kid being slapped around, he knew not to dare resist his mom, but he also knew he would not have to take any physical pain, too.

The truth of the matter is her type of behavior actually showed her lack of control over her son. A parent in complete control would have just said, go home I will deal with you later. And later at home she would have put two or three hard painful licks on his ass that would have really hurt.

I'm just glad I raised my kids over forty years ago; otherwise today I would be in jail.
SIRMANS LOG: 02 MAY 2015, 1305 HOURS.

IT'S A PHONY USA ECONOMY FOOL. WRITER LETS IT ALL HANG OUT IN DEEP, DEEP ANGER. It is getting to where I am writing more and more notes or very short one or two paragraph articles. The reason is I have mostly said it all that truly matters, and to say more is just mostly a waste of my time.

Very few want a taste of my bitter medicine. Seems my great wisdom will only be appreciated after a lot of unnecessary great pain and suffering takes place in this great country. A lot of people in the USA know we have lost our way.

They know the country is in serious trouble, and can't survive on its present course. We have a situation like the seven blind men examining an elephant. One thought the legs were tree trunks, and another thought the tail was a rope.

The USA economy and the whole inner moral and culture fabric of the country are coming apart at the seams. The conservatives bless their hearts, at least they are aware and can see the handwriting on the wall and want to stop the madness.

Whereas the liberals are too shallow to be aware of or even know the economy is in danger of totally collapsing from too much spending. The liberal are hell-bent on starving the military and social spending this great nation out of existence, period.

Sure, the conservatives are aware of the over spending danger and wants to do whatever it takes to save our country, but in my view they doesn't have the perspective to see the big picture and will wild goose chase down endless false paths.

However, this is where my great supernatural wisdom comes into play and sets me apart from all but a handful. "There is always more than one way to skin a cat." And there are countless ways of saving the USA. However, I believe I am one of a handful with the deep, deep perspective to actually see the moving parts to proper dissect the USA economy.

I have the ability to see that the evil 1938 socialist minimum wage law took the discipline out of the USA economy. That caused the USA economy to be a phony weak P.... of an economy ever since that day. That almost 80 years ago fatal mistake must first be corrected before it is even possible to think about saving the great USA.

The USA must have a strong disciplined economy first before it will ever be able to save our culture, morals, or the economy itself and in that same order. This is fact, I see it, and I know it, but how many in power even know this or will agree with me on this, none is the answer.

So be it, I can shout it on the mountaintop, but I can't make anyone hear me. I love my country, and I'm mad, and I'm angry, but I know I must calm myself and continue the emergency distress call for USA survival, that is my destiny.

SIRMANS LOG: 29 APRIL 2015, 2032 HOURS.

A 2016 PRESIDENTIAL ELECTION MIND BLOWING ANALYSIS

I ,Freddie L Sirmans Sr. believe the 2016 presidential election may become so polarized that hoards of Christians, independents, conservatives, etc. like never before will turnout and vote. November 2016 may be the most important United States election since 1776 in my view. It will determine if the United States survives as a free nation or survives at all, period.

I, great writer if I had any real sense I wouldn't touch this hot potato issue with a ten-foot pole, but knowing me I have no business being a writer in the first place. The Dem's and liberals knows they must win the 2016 presidential election at all cost, or the evil 1938 socialist minimum wage law may finally be repealed. "I wish, the last part I just threw that in there for my sake, y'all."

Sure, there are a lot of republican candidates going for the 2016 presidential gold, but I believe the real drama and action is going to be on the Dem's side. The reason I say this is I think the real movers and shakers on the Democratic side doesn't think Mrs. Clinton can win this milestone election.

Of course, no one over there is ever going to admit to anything of the sort. But, "you can bet your bottom dollar that ways and actions always speak louder than words." Folks, I'm a writer and could be totally wrong on this whole matter, I'm just writing what I believe.

Still, I think the long political knives are being sharpened within the Democratic Party. And before this 2016 presidential election is over a lot of Democratic political blood is going to be spilled. In 2016 for the Dem's and the sake of their power everything is on the line, even the welfare state itself, and believe me the knock out drag out is not going to be pretty, y'all.

The smart money thinks the republicans will keep control of both houses of congress in 2016. That means if the republicans win the 2016 presidency they will have a trifecta, which means the liberal and Democratic Party power monopoly starting with the "New deal" may finally be broken. Hallelujah. As you can see, all of the marbles are at stake for the liberals and Dem's. Myself, I see the dawning of a new day coming, people.

This is my one man's analysis of what's so much at stake here concerning this milestone 2016 election. We'll see, just how this real life soap opera ultimately plays out. Stay tuned.
SIRMANS LOG: 23 APRIL 2015, 1438 HOURS.

JUST A FEW WORDS OF WISDOM:
Economically wise, until our cruel evil 1938 socialist minimum wage law is repealed, no matter what the conservatives or the republicans do the game is still being played on a liberalism home court.

It is no longer a matter of if the great USA will be over powered by liberalism but how soon. If our phony hog-tied economy doesn't sink us first, we are already up to our neck in a vast moral decay and culture rotted liberalism swamp and the only relief in sight is repealing our evil 1938 socialist minimum wage law. But, I seem to be the only one with the God given wisdom to see the light on this, I pound and I pound, only to thick sculls and deaf ears.

So be it, I have filled my destiny and done my duty. I will start closing by saying this: Many people have endured great pain and suffering and said "They were actually glad it happened because it opened their eyes to things right before them that they could never see before." That is what has happen to the great USA, our liberal induced welfare state has lulled almost everyone asleep, the nation will just have to experience the pain and suffering and learn the hard way if the nation survives.

The prevailing thinking today is government owes us a living and is responsible for the people's survival. However, nothing could be further from the real truth, it is just the opposite. The people or private enterprise is responsible for the survival of government not the other way around; government is a parasite and can't survive unless the people support it.

The USA government is taking from 40 percent of the people and using that seized profit to take care of the other 60 percent of the people. Plus, we will soon be over 20,000,000,000,000,000,000 in debt and counting. Now, if anyone thinks this can last very much longer you are a dumb ignorant fool in my view.

SIRMANS LOG: 21 APRIL 2015, 0005 HOURS.

COLD REALITY CHECK:
Sure, anyone with an ounce of economic sense should know that the reasonable answer to the USA economy problem is to first balance the budget. But, the cold reality is the liberals have made so many voters government dependent that it is political suicide for any individual or political party to dare go there, and expect to remain in power.

It is just impossible to balance the USA budget without creating a smaller pie, which in the short run is going to cause some extra pain. And guess what, to hell with what's best down the road, what have you done for me lately is all that's going to matter in the voting booth for the masses of government dependents.

Obviously, politically no political party is ever going to be able to balance the budget to get control of the USA economy, period. However, no political party may be able to balance the budget but a true free market place economy definitely can.

Not only can a true free market place economy balance the budget, it will send liberalism packing and take our country back from all of these shallow minded do-good talking heads with weak survive instincts. The only true answer to saving the USA is not about getting lost on our phony hog-tied economy, immigration, or our insane foreign policy; it is about repealing the 1938 minimum wage law.

That will set free our hog-tied USA economy, then the economy will have the force and power to kick ass, send liberalism packing, balance the budget, and do what ever it take to save this great nation of individual freedom. Otherwise, there is not going to be a USA.

Take that as a dose of cold reality, writer, Freddie L Sirmans Sr. style. How do you like me now?
SIRMANS LOG: 10 APRIL 2015, 2228 HOURS.

Freddie L Sirmans Sr. weight losing helpful hint using the "Positive thinking" technique.
The definition of the positive thinking technique I'm talking about is: One takes a short saying or quote and repeats it over and over to ones self a minimum of fifty times or more every day.

It may take up to six months or more to start feeling strong results. This is the quote I use: "I can keep my body slim and healthy through God who strengthens me." Just leave God off or substitute another deity if one doesn't believe in God.

Lets face it folks, some of us like me are compulsive over eaters; I have suffered with this disorder ever since I was a child. Some of us just simply can't do it alone, that is why turning to God by saying through God who strengthens me is all-powerful.

However, it doesn't work over night, it takes a while to break through to the subconscious. But, if one stays the course long enough positive results will be realized.

Salt and sodium are the biggest factors in controlling high blood pressure. I buy the gallon jugs of drinking water with 0 sodium. Also, I buy the little squeeze bottles of fresh lemon juice and drink lemon water as my main beverage, no sugar added for me. I believe some water is loaded with sodium for the same reason as processed foods, be aware.

NOTE:
There is a simple universal fact about life and survival, risk and struggle is a greater part of it. If too much risk and struggle is taken out of life, then its purpose and value greatly diminishes. It is in our DNA from evolving over the eons. Repealing our evil 1938 socialist minimum wage law will rescue the USA from our dying liberal welfare state, which has made the USA a P.... of a society.

LIBERAL SUICIDE SPENDING
This is a subject I decided to revisit. There is a conservative faction that wants to bring about a states convention to demand the government balance it's annul budget.

On the surface having a convention to do that sounds reasonable and maybe ought to take place. Twenty years ago I probably would have jumped on the bandwagon. However, I have evolved and now realize liberalism has no boundaries or limits to what it will go to keep over spending.

Today I think any convention of the sort would more than likely cause a total disaster. The first reason is it wouldn't solve the problem. Our welfare state beast is ignoring the constitution and the law now and just adding new laws are not going to make this beast change its ways. The next reason involves human nature.

Liberals tends to be far more intelligent and smarter than conservatives but as a rule are shallow surface dwelling thinkers. The conservative's advantage has always been their focused staying power and deep sound judgment. However, there is a world of difference between today's conservatives and those in the founding fathers days.

Ever since the "New deal" and the come about of our welfare state conservatives has become almost as moral corrupted and shallow minded as liberals. It is a waste of time to pass more laws trying to force liberals to control spending.

They have weak survival instincts and respects no threats in spending from here to kingdom come. But, never forget liberals are not dumb or stupid, when giving up any of their own money they are the stingiest of any group. What it actually boils down to is they struggle with not being selfish to a fault, and that includes spending other people money.

Most conservatives are self-bound by morals and emotional boundaries such as guilt, shame, etc. Where as liberals tends to be far less restricted when going after something they truly want. Nothing that is within the law is going deter a liberal lion/lionness from grabbing power and keeping it.

Power is what this liberal suicide spending is all about. Social spending keeps liberals in power and no amount of morals; love of the country, or anything legal is going to stand in their way of holding on to power. Many liberals tend to be aimless but you give a liberal a cause or a goal and you got an almost unstoppable force on your hand.

If the great USA is to ever get control over suicide over spending from the liberals it can only be done with a physical barrier. So, here we go again, that means repealing the 1938 minimum wage law. Enacting that law is what took away a government-spending barrier in the first place.

That law gave liberals absolute power over private enterprise and private property rights and enable them to tax spend inflate, tax spend inflate, tax spend inflate in a never-ending upward spiral. In fact I don't believe its possible for any free nation to remain free very long with liberalism and liberals at the helm.

Freedom and democracy demands a responsible and self-controlled populace to last over a hundred years in my view. The liberals seized complete control over USA private business enterprise and private property rights with the enacting of the 1938 minimum wage law.

Unless that law is repealed this nation will never remain free to 2038 let alone more than a hundred years since the law was enacted.
SIRMANS LOG: 02 APRIL 2015, 2107 HOURS.

CAN THE USA ECONOMY AVOID TOTAL CHAOS IF THE ECONOMY COLLAPSES

I felt like doing some thinking out loud on paper on how much time the country have before our economy totally collapses. I will try to make this article short and not get carried away.

I will start by saying anyone with an ounce of economic wisdom should know that this madness can't possibly be sustained. No one knows how or when all of this economic madness is going to finally play out in the end, not even me.

But, I do know two things our welfare state is about to butt heads on. Number one is the days of our welfare state in the role of social and family provider is over, the government just doesn't realize it yet.

The other thing is our welfare state beast will never surrender it power of being a social and family provider even if it means giving up our sovereignty, selling off the country, or whatever to hold on that role.

It is a role the government should never have been in from the start. Government in the role of super provider is like feeding on itself or eating its young. Nature's law of taking the course of least resistance can be extremely disarming and seductive.

That is because no caring and reasonable person wants to see suffering and hardship. But, like drugs, sex, gambling, and anything that gives relief and pleasure, too much of a good thing can be a trap.

While good men and women stood by the shallow minded liberals with good intent eased the government into a permanent role of being a social and family provider. This is a role that for over 6,000 years had always been with the nuclear and extended family head of household.

I'm sure over the centuries governments had tried playing daddy before but before it had always failed. And the only reason it hasn't failed so far in the USA is because of our evil 1938 socialist minimum wage law. That evil law is what has kept this farce going this long.

The evil 1938 minimum wage law has allowed the liberals to grow government unabated by inflating our currency to no end. And they call it growing the economy, which it is not; it is sheer madness and insanity in my view. Sure, this insanity can work for around four generations then it's going to be hell to pay.

That is because ever since this insanity started around 80 years ago it has rotted away the tools and foundation that allows for an organize society to exist. The tools I am referring to are a strong nuclear and extended family system, and an adequate supply of small farmers and home gardeners. That would provide some emergency backup bartering capacity to buy time in case the economy collapses and money was worthless.

In term of long-term survival nothing can take the place of the strong nuclear and extended family system. Without the strong nuclear family system not enough men and women of sound judgment can be produced to maintain an orderly responsible society.

Only the strong nuclear family will make sure proper norms and traditions are instilled in the very young. Experienced wisdom, good morals, and spiritual values must be instilled and passed on or chaos will eventually result.

Sure, living in a world of plenty with full stomachs most of us are so caring with good intentions that we never wake up to smell the coffee. But, I'm here to tell you that we Americans along with much of the industrialized world below the surface are spoiled rotten.

We are comfortable and living in a dream, not knowing that we have almost no tools to survive on when this mad insane economy soon collapses. Without the umbrella of a strong nuclear and extended family system very few are going to make great self-sacrifices for greedy selfish thankless strangers. And self-sacrificing is what it will take to survive as a nation during severe hard and tough times.

However, all of this coming doom can be avoided by repealing the evil 1938 socialist minimum wage law. Even repealing the 1938 minimum wage law is going to cause much pain and hardship but it will be controllable and not turn into chaos.

Once the USA economy is free and unshackled it won't take much to eat and survive, and there is nothing more powerful on earth than a genuine true free market economy. There is no doubt in my mind it will save the USA and western civilization. And may the Gods smile down on this great nation.

P.S.
A non minimum wage genuine true free market place economy won't allow inflation and a phony currency for very long, like a liquid a true free market place economy will soon seek its own level.
SIRMANS LOG: 29 MARCH 2015, 0101 HOURS.

THE WORLD WOULD BE A COLD DREARY PLACE WITHOUT LIBERALISM

I'm going to briefly say a few words on liberalism. Sure, I criticize liberalism as much as anyone but I love liberals as well as all people. The world would be a cold dreary existence without liberals and liberalism, who else would guarantee that Bamba is safe and the soft emotional side of life prevails.

However, there has never been and never will be a society that survives very long with liberalism at the helm. The evil 1938 socialist minimum wage law allowed liberalism to gain control of the USA government. And ever since layer by layer they have been running this great USA ship of state aground.

Liberals have a weak survival instinct and can't see any danger in spending this nation out of existence. They have no concept of the pain, suffering, and turmoil that will result from a collapsed economy due to reckless spending. Plus, on the other hand the liberals have made far too many people government dependent for Republicans to succeed in trying to balance the USA budget.

That approach will surly fail for two main reasons; the first reason is it will definitely create a smaller economy pie, which in the short run will make the economy worse. The second reason is the liberal media and general public is economically ignorant and living in the now and could care less about what is best down the road.

So, when the pie starts getting smaller and painful the Republicans will be booted out of office short order. I think the republicans should just tread water until after November 2016, then do the deed I have been advocating.

Now, I will say again what I have said a thousand times or more, if the republican wants to save this great nation, repeal the evil 1938 socialist minimum wage law, period. That will set free our shackled free market place economy. And there is nothing on earth more powerful than a genuine true free market place economy.

If the republicans set our economy free all they will need to do is be still, the true free economy will take it from there and save this great nation for our children and grand children. However, I'm a realist, I know anything I say, just the opposite will be done, so be it.

In my view there is nothing innate about being a liberal, that is why before our welfare state it was almost unheard of to find a poor liberal. Before our welfare state our poor always had the strongest morals, they could be trusted to work in ones home and very few would take an unborn life.

Today, one poor minority group in the USA are killing the unborn at a higher rate than anywhere in the world. The fact is if any nation is to survive long term Liberalism must never be allowed to completely takeover.

However, there is no denying it; ever since the "New deal" and the 1938 minimum wage law liberalism has dominated the USA government, period. Liberalism, some of it is in the stars but environment always over rules that, which is why I am totally convinced that only repealing the 1938 minimum wage law can break the liberalism death choke hold on this nation.

Liberalism at our helm is like having a kid behind the wheel. Plus, our liberal welfare state has destroyed our culture and morals, but the most deadly of all, it has destroyed our sense of sound judgment. Survival then becomes a far more risky business, sort of like the roll of the dice, or not even dealing with a full deck.
SIRMANS LOG: 26 MARCH 2015, 1414 HOURS.

THE FOLLY OF THINKING THE USA BUDGET CAN BE BALANCED???

A genuine true non-phony free market place economy without exception must be able to set its own wages and prices, period. The liberals in charge of the government seized that right when they enacted the evil 1938 socialist minimum wage law.

That act castrated the USA economy and has led to the destruction of our culture and morals. And until the

USA economy is given back its power by repealing the evil 1938 socialist minimum wage law nothing can break the liberals choke hold on this great nation. Otherwise, there is simply no way this great nation of individual freedom can ever be saved.

Men and women of sound mind with strong survival instincts must give the USA economy back its true power, that way it can save this great nation. Nothing else has the power and discipline to drain this vast liberal swamp and prevent individual freedom from disappearing off the face of the earth forever. God save the USA the last bastion of true individual freedom left in the world today.

The truth of the matter is government is actually a parasite; it can only survive if it has a host to take from. Government is not part of the economy but what it does greatly affects the economy. Every society must have a means of protecting itself from internal and external threats and dangers, and that makes having some form of government a must.

Most governments have the power to take over that is why most private sector host has strong built in protections and total control over the money supply. But, like they say, "The way to hell is paved with good intentions."

On the surface the government doing good and helping people doesn't seem like a threat, and it is not in perspective on a temporary basis. But, in reality government must never become a social and family provider more than on a temporary basis if a free nation is to survive long term.

Whoever is the provider is the boss like it or not. That is why in the USA and Western Europe for all practical purpose the welfare state has taken over. Today there are far too many people dependent on the government to ever put government spending on a diet.

In Western Europe and now in the USA the money priority first goes to the welfare state over the military and all else. And there is only contempt for the profit driven private business enterprise host. Plus, private business days may be numbers because liberal media and the masses don't understand profit and hate it.

Still, there is a savior waiting on a white horse ready to ride in to rescue western civilization. But first, the evil 1938 socialist minimum law must be shot with a silver bullet or a stake driven through its heart by repealing or getting rid of all minimum wage laws entirely. This evil poison pill law must be buried to never rise again for any democracy to ever be safe.

In terms of raw bare boned survival using good intentions and doing the right thing may cause Mother Nature to spit in your face. Just look at the animal kingdom with raw nature, there is no place for good intentions or doing the right thing, except to starve.

Now, you look at the USA economic situation, from a political point of view good intentions and doing the right thing I believe will surely get you booted out of power, period. Folks, let me stop right here and explain, I'm a writer and I write it as I see it. I can be wrong, in fact I hope I am wrong on some of the dire things I see coming down the pike.

I have said it before and am going to say it again, anyone that still thinks the USA and western Europe can be saved as welfare states is economically ignorant in my view. Maybe I'm the one who is ignorant. However, I believe I can dissect and understand the inner workings of an economy as well as anyone.

Yet, for the life of me I can't see any social and family provider welfare state doing anything but slowly devouring its own survival host, which is private business enterprise. Economically, it is just impossible for a welfare state to survive very much longer by constantly dwindling its own only survival host, which is profit driven private business enterprise.

Government can take only so much profit before there is none left to take. Anyone with common sense should know that the USA can't forever reckless spend and keep going deeper and deeper into debt. A reasonable person should conclude that the right thing to do is balance the budget and get your physical house in order.

Sure, that is the responsible thing to do if you are talking about around 80 years ago right after the minimum wage law was enacted. But, today for a political party to take that type of normal responsible action is political suicide.

Now, here is where my super wisdom comes into play. OK, lets just imagine that at the snap of fingers all of the USA debts are paid free and clear, do you think the health of the nation would be solved? My answer would be no! Our debt is a currency problem but civilization existed long before a currency was invented.

The main problems with the USA and western civilization are culture and moral in my view. Contrary to the common view I believe in free nations the economy is the real disciplinarian that actually guards and protects the nations culture and morals.

Sure, we are a nation ruled by law not by man, but I believe the economy is the real power that pulls the strings behind the scene. Also, I believe liberalism is actually what's destroying the USA, which could never have happen with a genuine true free market place economy.

I feel the economy the USA has today is a phony P.... of an economy and has been that way ever since the evil 1938 minimum wage law was enacted. The economy the USA has today doesn't have the power or discipline to protect itself or the nation's culture and morals.

Once the 1938 minimum wage law was enacted, that allowed liberalism a foot in the door to inflate the currency and grow government to no end. Since then the minimum wage law gave government absolute power over prices and wages. Once that happened the aggressive liberals has played to the basic weaknesses in our human nature by promising the moon and back.

The minimum wage law gave government complete control over private property rights and private business enterprise, which it had never had before in the history of the country. By repealing the minimum wage law the economy would regain its power to guard and protect the nations culture and morals, plus boom the economy in real growth not any phony inflated growth like today.

So, the republican think they can take on our welfare state beast and balance the budget, plus remain in power. Well, I'm one that thinks they are in for a very rude awakening. I hope I'm wrong, but I think the beast will defend itself and win. I truly feel only a genuine true free market place economy minus any minimum wage law has the power and ability to take down this beast.

They will never agree with me, but I feel the only wise course the republicans has left to save the USA is to repeal the evil 1938 socialist minimum wage law, "That is all she wrote." As to liberals saving the country, they are the ones hell bent on destroying it and too shallow to even realize it.
SIRMANS LOG: 17 MARCH 2015, 1748 HOURS.

IS THE USA ENTERING A TOTAL BREAKDOWN OF ITS SOCIETY?
You can't get blood out of a turnip. And you can't have a peaceful and orderly society without strong discipline. So, in my view the USA is entering a totally break down of our p.... of a society.

In authoritarian societies brute muscle power and force can be used to maintain discipline. Whereas in free societies people have individual rights and laws that must be obeyed to maintain strong discipline. But, in a free society when there is no brute power and force to maintain discipline two things is a must to prevent a total breakdown of that society.

Those two must things are first a genuine true free market place economy and second a strong nuclear and extended family system. A nations economy trumps everything because everyone must have food and warmth to survive. That is the reason immigration is out of control our welfare state allows our poor and uneducated to avoid doing hot hard work to keep the nation fed.

Somebody gotta do that type work or we all will starve. Now, you try to convince a farmer with his harvest rotting in the field that I'm wrong. Next is the nuclear family, there never has and never will be a society that last very long without a strong nuclear and extended family system.

It is almost impossible to maintain an orderly and peaceful society without making sure the very young are taught proper norms and traditions. That is what happen to the black community, the black man right out of slavery enforced and maintained discipline in the home.

He made sure proper norms and traditions were instilled in the very young before he was kicked out of the home by the welfare state. The welfare state never concerned itself with proper behavior and to this day is still financing its destruction.

Many people are worried about the government completely taking over, well, with the way things are falling apart, the day may come when the people rise up and demand the government take over. **SIRMANS LOG: 12 MARCH 2015, 2229 HOURS.**

ABOUT THIS NET NEUTRALITY TROJAN HORSE GIFT

I, great writer Freddie L Sirmans Sr. decided to briefly comment on this "Net Neutrality" thing. The fact is I haven't read hardly anything or listen to very much about it on radio or TV. Still, I decided to weigh in on it anyway.

The truth is what they do don't bother me much one-way or the other. In many ways I feel the world would be better off if the Internet would never have been invented, but its here and anyone standing in the way of progress will get ran over.

I don't need details because I know once the government gets its greed little tax grubbing hands on the throat of the Internet it is ruined forever. It will end up just like our ruined health care system, and screwed up with very few able to afford it.

Before the government seized control of our USA health care system the poor and middle class could pay out of pocket their doctor visits and not over run the nations emergency rooms. Right now, most people don't need the Internet to survive, and the vast majority goes about their daily lives without it. But, once the government seizes enough control over it all of that is going to come to screeching halt.

Our welfare state beast is already slobbering and licking its chops seeing the Internet as a cash cow. They are going to make it where you can't get any kind of health care, a job, or anything else without going on line.

Right now the problem is no one knows how the Internet is going to be taxed, but I assure you the Internet will be made where you can't survive without it or paying to use it.

Warning, I'm fixing to go on a rant and it is my one-man belief and opinion, nothing more. Cease now, or continue reading at your own risk. So, if you want to know what I really think about our future, I may be wrong, but I think the USA will be fortunate if it survive 2015 without a totally economic collapse. And if we survive 2015 this economic lying and insanity can't possibly last much longer.

This is cold hard reality stuff, I just hope they don't start banning or burning my books. I believe that almost everything the USA government puts out concerning our current phony p…. of an economy is propaganda, period. I know beyond a shadow of a doubt that only repealing our evil 1938 socialist minimum wage law entirely can save the USA at this late stage.

Sure, I'm going to be dismissed as a nut case or kook and ignored for now. But, hate me; disagree with me or whatever, I know with my great supernatural wisdom history will prove me right without a doubt. Praise be to God. All of this economic insanity and madness is about to come to a head in my view.

I believe there is an energy or force governing the universe, you can call it God, a superior being, mother nature, natural selection, destiny, or whatever, but it maintains a balance in the universe and prevents total disorder.

Every action has a reaction counter part, every positive has a negative counter part, and every good has an evil counter part and vice-versa. Only balance maintains order in the universe. And it affects everything that exists, it is sort of like the whole universe is a unit of one. It is like good and evil is two sides of the same coin.

I will close with this, if you really want to understand and know how an economy and free market place is suppose to work read Freddie L Sirmans Sr. books if you can take it.

It saddens me to say this but western civilization has almost become a modern day Sodom and Gomorrah. So, guess what, the universe is beginning to adjust and balance all this same sex marring and mass murdering in the womb with??? You figure it out!!! I know but I will remain mute.

All human emotions evolved to aid human survival in some way. The negative emotions such as evil, hate, etc. are primarily geared to destroy in some way. So, in the eyes of nature there is no such thing as a good or bad emotion they are all just tools in maintaining a balance to keep order in the universe.

I believe when you see evil, evil seemingly like everywhere it is to counter balance something parading as good that is as equal threatening to human survival. My guess is evil is being balanced against the threats to procreation to aid human survival in some way. The process of procreation is in grave danger in the USA and western civilization and Mother Nature is stepping in.

In the USA and Western Europe there is mass means of birth control on demand, mass abortions and killing in the womb on demand, and now we are on a fast path to mass same sex marriages on demand. Now, if you don't think that is a moral and grave threat to procreation and the survival of our species, you are an ignorant fool with a weak survival instinct. Yet, you are the norm, this is what the liberal induced welfare state has brought us to.

Again, disagree if you will, I'm warning you, only removing or repealing the evil socialist minimum wage laws entirely from the USA and western economies can save western civilization from total doom. That is the only thing that can drain this vast liberal swamp. There are just too many two-faced anti-survival monsters dwelling in this self-gratification do-good-er swamp to contend with, the S.O.B. must be drained if the USA is to survive, period.

SIRMANS LOG: 24 FEBRUARY 2015, 1738 HOURS.

THE END

ENJOY BOLD RAW UNCUT CREATIVE WRITING BY NEUROTIC SELF-MADE WRITER FREDDIE L SIRMANS SR.

PURCHASE OR READ EXCERPTS BY VISITING HIS WEBSITE AT:
www.FLSirmans.com

The Trump Impact In 2016

www.ingramcontent.com/pod-product-compliance
Lightning Source LLC
Chambersburg PA
CBHW022112210326
41521CB00028B/315